About this book In *Terminal Architecture* Martin Pawley argues that art history is what stops us understanding architecture. He believes that the real barometer of the value of buildings today is not their aesthetic pedigree, but their usefulness as terminals in the maze of communications and distribution networks that sustain modern life.

Pawley contends that because we use the wrong system to value our buildings we send the wrong signals to the people who plan our cities. As a result urban life is being destroyed by politicians, planners, art historians and the heritage and tourist industries, all of them ignoring network thinking in favour of fake historicism, crumbling infrastructure, phantom populations, no-go areas and increasingly restrictive security measures. As a result authentic architecture has become disurbanized. It survives only in the shape of buildings like distribution centres, factories and petrol stations that are designed as instruments, not monuments.

The vision described in *Terminal Architecture* is apocalyptic. It predicts what will follow architecture and the city. It cannot fail to stimulate debate.

About the author Martin Pawley is a former architecture critic of the *Guardian* and the *Observer*. He studied architecture in Oxford, Paris and London and is the author of several books on the subject including *Building for Tomorrow* (1982); *Theory and Design in the Second Machine Age* (1990); *Buckminster Fuller: a biography* (1991) and *Future Systems* (1993). He was editor of the magazine *World Architecture* for several years.

Terminal Architecture

Martin Pawley

REAKTION BOOKS

Published by Reaktion Books Ltd
11 Rathbone Place
London W1P 1DE, UK

First published 1998

Series design by Humphrey Stone

Printed and bound in Great Britain by
Biddles Limited, Guildford, Surrey

British Library Cataloguing in Publication Data:

Pawley, Martin
   Terminal Architecture. – (Essays in art and culture)
   1. Architecture
   I. Title
   720

   ISBN 1 86189 018 4

Contents

Introduction

*'Man is a knot, a web, a mesh into which relationships are tied.
Only those relationships matter. The body is an old crock that nobody
will miss. I have never known a man to think of himself when dying.
Never.'*

ANTOINE DE SAINT EXUPÉRY
Wind, Sand and Stars, 1939

The title of this book, *Terminal Architecture*, is a play on the
meaning of 'terminal', a word that is applicable to the state of
architecture both now and in the future. At present it relates to
the way in which the cultural role of architecture – nurtured by
the art-historical shibboleths of individual genius, permanent
value and appropriateness of style – is utterly divorced from
the practical need for the production of buildings. Contemporary architecture can be described as 'terminal' because a
gross lack of correspondence of this order is equivalent to the
lack of connection between disease and cure when a hospital
patient no longer responds to treatment. Such a patient is said
to be in a 'terminal' condition.

There is, however, a second way in which the word 'terminal' can be applied, for not only does the word dismiss an
old interpretation of architecture, it welcomes a new way of
looking at it after it is stripped of its art-historical trappings.
According to this second use of the word, the 'terminal'
descent into meaninglessness of architecture's old value
system does not signify the end of all architecture (which is
self-evidently all around us, indifferent to the fate of all the
theories that describe it, and resistant to everything short of a
nuclear war). Instead it signifies the beginning of a new
enlightenment, an awareness that the act of building can be
better understood, and valued, as the provision of 'terminals'
for the systems and networks that sustain modern life, rather
than as the creation of cultural monuments.

Following these trains of thought, two quite different
images of the state of architecture can be illuminated by the
single word 'terminal'. The first, which might be termed the
'Terminal 1' vision, can best be imagined as something like a

religious painting, wherein the art-historical notion of architecture is conducted to its grave by professors, practitioners, arts administrators, critics and journalists, all of whom have come to the end of their capacity to find in it any signs of life. The second, which might be termed 'Terminal 2', conjures up a brash piece of machine art, an abstract tartan grid made up of overlaid networks whose connecting points, or 'terminals', are marked by simple coloured circles, like stations on a map of the London Underground. Every one of these circles represents a terminal of the future and a funeral of the past. The meaning of the second image is contained in the mass of intersecting lines and the networks they represent.

Like the great Millennium computer fault – the realization in the early 1990s that hundreds of thousands of commerical computer systems would have to be altered to prevent all their calendar references being thrown into error by the arrival of the double zero in 2000 – these two images offer a preview of the sudden breakdown of art history when attacked along such unconventional lines. By such means can the 'Terminal 1' funerary scene be transformed into a 'Terminal 2' operating system capable of energizing a new architecture.

The first chapter in this book is an attempt to describe, by means of a short story, what an architecture of terminals instead of art-historical masterpieces might be like. The combination of 'big shed' architecture with the abandonment of roads and the survival of the Ideal Home Show is a foretaste of the strangeness of life a century ahead, when our perception of normal and abnormal will not so much be different as rearranged out of ingredients that we already know. In this way 'Terminal 2098' is a starting point for the chapters that follow. These chapters deal in turn with the post-Cold War explosion of reality-simulating technologies and the marketing of reality as a commodity capable of replacing real estate; with the disappointments associated with a generation of high-rise building in London; with the triumphant migration of the commercial skyscraper to the Far East; with the power and culpability of art history; with the transition from Modern to post-Modern architecture; with the advent of terrorism as a force in urban planning and design; and with the concept of the urbanism of the sand-heap as the ultimate destination of our long-wave drift towards global population dispersal. The book ends with examples of post-urban Terminal Architecture that already exist, buildings differentiated by electronic means and devoid of art-historical significance.

This last qualification is important, for today hundreds of thousands of assessments of property value are made on the basis of art-historical judgements. As many, perhaps, as the computer calendar references that once depended upon the two-digit code used by the programmers of thirty years ago. The 'Terminal 1' value system, with its parade of Old Masters and young geniuses, carries a massive baggage of invest-ment, law and custom with it wherever it goes. Behind its beloved collection of derelict banks and 'at risk' churches, its 'saved' country houses, ancient telephone boxes, disused power stations and 'historically representative' local authority tower blocks, lies a whole social order that would be cast into the outer darkness by the triumph of 'Terminal 2' thinking. The resultant shock could scarcely be less profound than that threatened by European Monetary Union. It would involve a dramatic shift from the worship of the culture of enclosure, to the belated recognition that the hidden networks that pro-vide us with transport, energy, nutrients and information are the real riches of the modern world. In the course of this shift, whole edifices of preconception would tumble. The idea of the city as an unique treasure house would give way to the idea of the city as a state of communication, wherein the awe we today accord to the unique original would be transferred to the infinitely reproducible replica, and we should all be the richer for it.

Martin Pawley
Somerton, 1997

1 Terminal 2098

If you want a guided tour of the house of the future you have to book early, said the message on the monitor. The photographer and I looked at one another. There was an error of *100* years in the programme. Laughing, I punched the keys and asked for a booking. The monitor didn't even blink. It just asked matter-of-factly for our ID numbers. We punched those in too and waited again. After a moment the fax started groaning.

'It took the booking!' we exclaimed, half amazed, half amused. It was like keyboarding your way into the computer system of your own bank by accident, and then wondering if you really had done it. But there were the press passes coming off the fax. 'Good for twelve hours only,' said the overprinting. 'Please enter and leave by the car park entrance at 836559. Have a nice day.'

836559 was a map reference in Dorset. It took a day or two to set up our trip, and an overnight drive to get there. By the time we arrived we were already deeply sceptical. But there it was, an empty carpark with an entrance and the ticket booth illuminated by our headlights. It must have been about 5 a.m. and still dark when we fed our passes into the machine. We half expected them to be rejected, but no. The turnstile hummed and we pushed our way through. As far as we could see, we were the only visitors. Nobody was on duty at the ticket booth. There was only a big illuminated signboard saying 'To the terminals'. We stood there, one foot in each century so to speak, not knowing where to start. In the end we decided to wait for it to get light to see whether we were being taken for fools.

'Great shapes,' said the photographer, finally. He had been peering through the gloom using his 600mm lens like a telescope. I swung my binoculars in the same direction. The sun was just rising. We watched as it slowly illuminated a cluster of huge, low buildings. As soon as it was light enough we began to make our way on foot towards them. The ground was hard and dusty, sculpted into inexplicable ruts and ridges that ran like railway lines in all directions. Here and there bundles of cables snaked across our track, half buried, half exposed. We must have stepped over a thousand cables that morning, all just lying on the ground.

There were no trees between us and the settlement. Where we were, on the flat Dorset plain, there was just greyish vegetation in sprawling mounds that we instinctively avoided even though it meant detouring from our path. Once we stopped and listened carefully near one of these belts of weeds. It seemed to us we could hear a deep humming and wailing coming from it like a kind of music. There was even some suggestion of movement underneath. The photographer made as if to step into the biomass and suddenly a dog barked. Then others joined in. All their barking was identical and there seemed to be dogs all around us. Synchronized dog-barking. A strange and eerie sound. We backed away from the weed belt and it stopped; we advanced again and it started. The photographer noticed something like a lawn sprinkler sticking up from the edge of the weeds. One by one the dogs stopped. The lawn sprinkler retracted. Then the photographer reached down towards it and it shot out again and started to bark. We looked at one another and smiled nervously. A security system. After that we gave the weed belts a wide berth.

Twenty more minutes of tediously circuitous walking brought us to another obstacle, a series of low mounds of discarded containers and packaging arranged by the wind into fantastic sand dunes of waste flagged by torn and fluttering plastic sheets. Once again it was possible to move through, rather than over, these man-made barkhans by snaking along the ruts and ridges scored into the ground. Treading with special care over the uneven surface, we picked our way among the mounds like holidaymakers avoiding rocky outcrops on a beach. As we got closer to the big sheds we had seen from afar, the mounds of waste seemed to get bigger. Bleached and desiccated by the sun, we could see that they actually reached right up the shed walls and in some cases swept over the shallow slopes of their roofs.

Another five minutes found us walking over rutted ground between the sheds themselves; great monsters with sides 200 metres long, all arranged in a cluster around an access route marked out by an even greater concentration of ruts and ridges than we had seen before. It would be hard to exaggerate how difficult it was to walk in that territory. In the distance the access route led out over an elliptical concrete bridge under which lay a collection of what looked like shipping containers surrounded by more heaps of empty beverage cans, bottles and packaging, and partially hidden from view. Nearer to us, on the exposed side of the nearest shed, some huge lettering could still be seen. 'Z..US..' could still be made out in flaking black patches worn grey by the wind.

'Hi there,' said a voice suddenly, 'are you the long-distance bookings?' We looked around but could see nobody. The photographer shouted out that yes we were. At this a figure disengaged itself from the shadows that still lingered around the corners of the big sheds.

'My name's Carlos,' he said. 'I'm your guide to Ideal Home 2098. Any questions you have, just ask me. It's my job to make sure you see everything you want to see and still have time to have some fun.' Although he must have been 100 metres away Carlos's voice sounded almost intimately close. We later found out it was electronically projected. He advanced towards us with an eager stride. When he arrived I was the one who asked him the obvious question.

'Where are the houses of the future?'

'Houses? Houses is a bad word,' he frowned. 'We don't say house any more, we say terminals. Ter-min-als. Houses is a shit word these days. It means something bad. What you called debit in your day?'

'Debit? You mean debt?'

'Yeah, debt, debit. You know, when they take it all away like in Charles III's time? We call that the Age of Boxes. All live in boxes. Now we have terminals. Terminals are much better than houses. Nobody can take your terminal away. You take your terminal away yourself.'

While he spoke we studied Carlos. He looked normal enough but he wore strange clothes. A one-piece garment that looked like an Airforce mechanic's overalls in shiny grey. The photographer took a picture of him. He laughed.

'No big deal,' he said.

'What do you call those clothes?'

'Terminal,' he replied, smiling. And while we watched he inflated his suit like an airbag and rolled over onto his back on the ground. The suit completely enclosed him but we could still hear his voice as clear as ever: it never changed, far or near, outdoors or in. It always had that boom of presence, as though the loudness button was always on. It always made him sound impressive. Carlos deflated his terminal airbag to its original size and he stood before us again.

'This is the smallest terminal we have. You can live in here for a day or two, maybe a week. A hundred channels HDTV, 3,000 hours minimax video. 300 Gigabytes of ROM, 150 RAM. 25 kilowatts of heat if you need it. Low radiation fog gun. Fully recyclable. Bet you never saw anything like it.'

We did not speak. 'Any questions, you ask me,' Carlos added.

The photographer said: 'That thing with the suit. Will you do that again?'

When Carlos had obliged I had a question too.

'Does everybody live in . . . suits like this?'

'No way. Everybody lives in a terminal, that's for sure, but you can set up a terminal anywhere and have it look like anything. The only requirement is that it should fit into the pattern of the image cascade during daylight hours.'

'What's the image cascade?'

'Well, you know, currently it's Heritage holograms, Listed style, per cent for art, Hammer films, anything in the Bible's OK.'

'You mean it has to conform to some sort of regulation appearance?'

'Yes, but that's no problem. It includes most things.'

'But this stuff round here doesn't look like anything. It's just heaps of rubbish and sheds.'

'It's still pretty early, right? You wait a bit, then you'll see. It won't look like this for long. At least not to us.'

'Can you show us a bigger, er, more typical terminal than your suit?'

'Well, like I said, we're still early, but I guess some of the demonstrators will be around.' He motioned us to follow him and led the way towards what looked like a bizarre cluster of giant wasps' nests clinging to the wall of one of the sheds. Bizarre, because when you got closer you could see they were a collection of miniature historic buildings welded to a collection of cars. Carlos stopped just beneath a 1:72 scale model of the Temple of Abu Simbel that looked as though it was indissolubly joined to a type of car we did not recognize.

'Jim lives here, he's pretty active.'

As we were later to learn, Jim's terminal was indeed bigger than most, but even so it was smaller than his car. It was stacked up off the ground on columns of old CD players glued on top of one another. When Jim's terminal was connected to his car like this it looked as though he might be able to stretch out full length in it, just.

Despite being active Jim seemed uncommunicative at first. He let us look into his dwelling, which resembled the cockpit of a fighter aircraft with a water bed in it. 'How can you live in here?' I asked. Jim looked mystified. 'Excuse me?'

'How can you live in here, there's no space.' Jim picked up an umbilical keypad and punched a button. Suddenly the vast Dolby hush of a great cathedral descended over the interior of his tiny capsule. The terminal's envelope had become a screen and a panorama of open desert stretched away in all directions. It was astounding. It might have been a hundred miles from wall to wall. If we had shouted, we would have heard echoes. 'Plenty of space,' said Jim phlegmatically, and eclipsed the image with his finger.

'Can you do that again?' asked the photographer.

'Let me get this straight,' I said to Carlos. 'Does everybody live alone like Jim, in these little trick boxes?'

'More or less. You have to remember everybody really wants to live alone, they always have. Only traditional houses made it impossible. Big houses, all heavy eh? Cost a fortune, can't get rid of it, can't sell it, can't even throw it away! I know the history! Everybody had a bad time. People without houses were the poor ones in those days. No homes. They had to live in boxes. But if you look back with hindsight, those boxes were the first terminals. All they did was take all the technology you had in your houses or flats a hundred years ago and make a house out of them. Not put the technology in a house, but make a house out of the technology. It's obvious really. That's how you get from a heavy house to a light terminal.'

'Are they called terminals because they are really just like big satellite TV sets, connected like computers to energy, information and . . .'

'Well, really the people are the terminals. But OK, yes, the terminals get all that and nutrients and fluids. Brain packs, virtual worlds, endless interactive movies, cable living, on the wire, that's what we've got.

Jim here lives in this Egyptian terminal and his car and it's like a vast cinema when he wants. He can drink in the Jumbotron in full sensurround.

Sometimes he spends days on end in here popping pills, watching and listening. He can paint out any outside noise with white sound, graze in the refrigerator, keep the picture steady, bring it all back, images of everything he ever did – or wanted to do. Better than sharing and arguing, killing and crowding. Think about it. What a rush! To have filmed your whole life. To remember and relive all the things you have ever done. To visualize and display all the things you have ever thought of. It beats cut-throat competition or sharing with other people, I tell you. Nearly nobody lives with anybody any more. You should know that. It started in your time, before your time, more and more people living alone, now everybody does.'

It turned out that Jim's terminal was nearly eleven years old. He had helped the video rental company sling it at night, fixed with tension cables into a tiny gap between two big storage sheds at Exit 16, and propped up with a load of obsolete electronic gear. He had been one of the first to set up his own terminal in the science park.

Some planners had come once in an armoured car to look for infringements, but by then there were already 30 or 40 terminals plugged in there, feeding off the electricity the distribution centres generated to keep their warehouse-loads of food and perishable goods from rotting. The terminals did not interfere with the coming and going of the freezer trucks, they just clung like parasites to the big structures that defined the landscape, making use of the air rights, as they used to say. You could tell the planners weren't exactly happy about Exit 16 but there wasn't a lot they could do, not without the army. It was happening everywhere. They say the video companies financed a lot of it. In the end the planners gave up and told the terminal dwellers they were going to set up a light village there to hide the place so that the terminals could stay. Now it was a quiet place – anyway it was at weekends. In the week you wouldn't really be able to see it.

'What's it like living in Dorset, Jim?' I asked. Once again he looked dazed. Carlos intervened.

'Terminal people don't think like that,' he said, giving Jim a wink. 'They've left all that stuff behind them. Time is a vast continuum for them. Just like space. Jim doesn't think about living in Dorset, he lives everywhere. Everywhere he can get sounds, images and temperatures of on his screen. It's what you used to call the top shelf.'

'How does Jim vote?'

Neither Jim nor Carlos answered. Then suddenly Jim remembered. 'The 24-hour consumption environment party,' he said proudly. 'There was one round here once. You just push a button.'

Then he began to try to tell us about one of the last documentaries he had ever seen, squeezed between the commercials at four o'clock in the morning, that had explained everything. The way he remembered it now, the whole continuum of life, space and terminals must have started in Charles III's time when they closed the motorways and evacuated the cities. But he was not used to talking much and he could not manage any more.

A lot of our time in 2098 had already been spent in and around Jim's capsule. The photographer and I were not eager to waste time. Standing outside I looked at the odd arrangement of Jim's porticoed tent, its exterior looking exactly like stone except that it flapped in the breeze where it was velcroed onto his car.

'How do you get your car out?' I asked finally. But Jim had had enough. Carlos explained that in 2098 cars and houses were part of the same mechanism. When you went out in your car, part *of your house went too. 'Mobile satellite of the home,' I wrote in my notebook.*

'Time to come with me,' said Carlos suddenly. 'They are all leaving now anyway.' We followed him to a black-windowed van with six big wheels to handle the rough terrain.

'Carlos, why did they close the motorways?' I asked.

'They were a mess,' said Carlos. 'Like houses, too big, too expensive, too old. It all got out of control. They just closed them down in 2025 and everybody drove directly to where they wanted to go.'

'What? Across country?'

'Of course, we all do that now. No houses. No roads. Terminals. Four wheel drives. ATVs. You know it makes sense.'

There was a long silence as we watched what was happening at Exit 16 that morning. Elsewhere in the science park other residents had started to stir. It was like a Western movie when the Indians suddenly rise up from the ground where they have hidden to ambush the cavalry. Now we could see what they were: all around the big sheds were strung bizarre collections of dwellings, part trucks or cars, part tents, part houses. As the sun strengthened they began to bulge and tear; the vehicle parts left the house parts and the house parts left the ground parts. Some whole houses lumbered across the rutted tracks leading to the bridge, their windscreen washers sweeping away the night's accumulation of grey dust. Other vehicles seemed no more than skeletons, dune buggies with refrigerators fixed to them and monster trucks with enormous tyres, waving satellite antennae. Thin monopostos (single-seat cars) with their drivers laid almost flat.

Then as the sun rose in the sky and the early morning departures petered out, with the click and rattle of a suddenly energized electric circuit the walls of the sheds began to change. Images danced and focused on their corrugated surfaces, working the waste dunes and the weed belt into a complex of high-resolution holograms that represented something we were utterly unprepared for: a scene of rural life out of Thomas Hardy. There were hayricks, fields of corn, grazing cows, and old cottages and barns. The desolate scene we had witnessed at dawn was now invisible. We could not see it. Nobody could see it. So it wasn't there. There was a light village there instead.

After the exodus, Carlos turned his 6x6 van out of the complex and began to head west, straight across countryside that had become a vast prairie. Occasionally we saw other vehicles travelling in other directions, but not often. The bits of road and motorway we crossed had small settlements of terminals on them. There was no through traffic any more. Yet the terminals all looked in the main like cars. In fact I noticed early on that Carlos always referred to the van as a terminal, like his suit, like Jim's capsule, like Jim. There were terminals everywhere, like digital clocks back in 1998. After a time our questions petered out. Our conversation was slowly dying of a surfeit of amazement.

As we rumbled along over wasted country from one nest of terminals to the next, we came to see that a great entropy had taken place in the hundred years since our own time. Many great problems that taxed our leaders in 1998 had just disappeared. The housing problem was no more because there were no houses; the population problem seemed to be unimportant because there were no marriages any more, no cohabitation and no children. The sex war was over because there were no competing genders, only individuals bound up in the study of their own personalities. As far as I could tell, you could not distinguish between women and men, they all looked like terminals. There was no society. No landscape to speak of. The way Carlos talked, it seemed as if machines produced everything all the time. Nobody bought anything, they just took it and then dumped it and took something else. Despite the ozone shields here and there nobody appeared to care much about pollution. There was no unemployment problem because nobody worked. When I asked about food, Carlos thought for a bit and then said that there were special farms in Ireland that fed the whole of Europe. As I stared out of the tinted windows I realized that our progress over this bland but uneven landscape was a paradigm for the future, as purposeful yet as meaningless as the noise of a tank, car or plane in a video game. Everything that had happened in a hundred years had already begun happening in our own time. Nothing was new. Everything was different.

In the whole of our journey we only saw the edge of one small town and that was Dorchester. Carlos did not think it was interesting.

'No one has driven in the towns for fifty years,' he scoffed, and that was that. All we could see from a hill to the west of the town were rows of houses that might have been 200 years old apart from the black glass in their windows and armoured front doors like submarine hatches. Among the houses an ancient tower with four pinnacles supported a giant dish antenna. Around and between the old houses crawled brightly coloured concertina tubes and roof-mounted pods and aerials. Cross streets were blocked off with more black glass and corrugated plastic, shipping containers were dumped *here and there. Everywhere those symbiotic car/terminals seemed to have plugged themselves onto the sides of houses like twentieth-century sculptures. Carlos said that all the old towns and cities were like this: decayed, ruined, their public buildings, office blocks, palaces and museums either abandoned or used as natural outcrops or caves to hang the ubiquitous terminals on. Because of high-definition interactive TV everybody could see everywhere and be everywhere. So everybody lived everywhere, or thought they did. Apart from Carlos at the very beginning of our visit, we never saw a single person on foot outdoors. But then, what we saw was not necessarily what was there, as the other 'light villages', with their spurious identities that we occasionally glimpsed – and which Carlos insisted were much more interesting – reminded us.*

After what must have been half an hour of travel, Carlos stopped his van by a stainless-steel sign that we would not have noticed ourselves. It was decorated with a rose symbol that reminded us of our own time. The incised lettering beneath it read 'Grade II* Heritage attraction ahead. Digital security system operating.'

'This is a big house,' said Carlos triumphantly. 'This is what I brought you to see. This one is rich. He is Nick the driver. He lives in the house of MGBs.'

This implausible assertion proved to be true for, when we headed in the direction indicated by the sign, we soon saw a great mound of metal ahead of us. To us it did not look like a house at all, more like a car breakers' yard from our own time, but Carlos insisted that this one really was a house, not a terminal, one of the very few houses left.

When we got out next to the mound we met its owner, Nick. Carlos treated Nick with great respect because, he said, Nick held the title of works driver. Works driver of Dorset. His grandfather had driven on the motorways before they had been closed down, and his great-grandfather had actually driven cars in the old cities. It was his grandfather who had begun the great collection of MGBs that Nick's father had allowed to decay. Some said that there had been more than 300 of them early in the century, but by the time Nick had the MGBs hauled into a large circle and piled up, a lot of them had rotted away. The ones that were left Nick had stacked up three storeys high, corbelling inwards like an Indian hogan. He had made windows out of collections of windshields glued together and had waterproofed the lot with transparent polymers sprayed from a mobile crane. Inside, Nick had built a kind of terminal stage-set of a home that was one of the largest in the West of England. He stood proudly inside his heap of MGBs, winding the window in the door of one slowly up and down while the photographer shot off a roll of film.

'This', said Carlos confidentially, 'is really historic, eh? This is the Ideal Home of 2098.' And he laughed as though he had rewarded us with the surprise that he knew we had been waiting for.

2 From Cold War to New Reality

*'I tell you these are great times. Man has mounted science,
and is now run away with. I firmly believe that before many centuries
more, science will be the master of man. The engines he will have
invented will be beyond his strength to control. Some day science may
have the existence of mankind in its power, and the human race will
commit suicide by blowing up the world. Not only shall we be able to
cruise in space, but I see no reason why some future generation
shouldn't walk off like a beetle with the world on its back, or give it
another rotary motion so that every zone should receive in turn its
due portion of heat and light.'*
HENRY ADAMS (1838–1918), American Ambassador to
Great Britain during the American Civil War

A century and a half before the Ideal Home Show of 2098 the
American art historian George Kubler wrote, in *The Shape of
Time*, 'If the accounting is correct, there can be no great causes
without great events.' And although he died before it came to
pass there is no doubt that one of the greatest events of recent
years, and the clearest demonstration of the truth of his
words, was the end of the Cold War. Global in its impact, the
repercussions of this event have ranged far and wide across
politics, philosophy and economics until it seems that no
aspect of the future will be untouched by it. From bankruptcy
and mass unemployment in the once lavishly funded science-
based industries of the former Soviet Union, to the transformation of America's Rockwell International Corporation
from a debt-laden B-1 bomber-maker to the debt-free manufacturer of 80 per cent of the fax modems in the world, bizarre
and unforeseeable transformations have lumbered in its wake,
so it is by no means foolish to argue that a whole conception
of reality ended with the Cold War, and thereafter a new state
of being took its place. What was perceived when the Cold
War ended was not a military triumph but a temporal one. A
vast planar present settled over past and future, converting
the once antagonistic East and West into the heads and tails of
a single coin. The Cold War may have been history's last
throw, but it was also the first throw of a post-historical era of
thought in which the ideas of the past could no longer be

made to define the categories of the present. In this sense it can be visualized as a kind of locked cold store wherein was preserved, along with many outdated ideologies, a treasure trove of technological ideas about the limits of perception, and an arsenal of mechanisms that could be used to so intensify it as to transform the nature of reality itself. The breaking open of this cold store changed the world.

In considering the events surrounding the collapse of the former Soviet Union, the reunification of Germany, the disintegration of the former Yugoslavia and all the geopolitical changes that pursued their domino effect around the world after the failure of the Socialist economic system, emphasis is invariably given to the military and political consequences. The unresolved economic consequences are considered to be a second-order phenomenon, still, as it were, in a state of adjustment. This may be correct as far as the Olympian heights of government are concerned, but at ground level a whole spectrum of civilian industries was affected by the transformation, just as much as were generals, admirals and international arms dealers. As the seismic shocks rippled through the world's economies, first the development industry, then the construction industry, and finally the architectural profession woke up to the meaning of the sea-change of 1989. For as well as throwing the military establishments and defence contractors of both sides into chaos, and bankrupting property companies from Tokyo to the Isle of Dogs, the lifting of the Iron Curtain opened up the possibility of a truly global market in building design services for the first time.

Until the end of the Cold War deregulated the world construction market it had been possible, in the separate economic zones of North America, the Middle East, the Far East and Eastern and Western Europe, for large design firms to survive within their own national boundaries and spheres of influence, safe from serious competition from overseas. After 1989 this kind of protectionism became much more difficult to sustain. Directly or indirectly the ramifications of the collapse of the Soviet economic trading area penetrated every construction market. Uncertainty led to dramatically reduced public sector spending in the mixed economies of the West, and plunging property prices everywhere followed the disintegration of the Comecon system. In the world of architecture, competition for work immediately became intense. Whenever competing

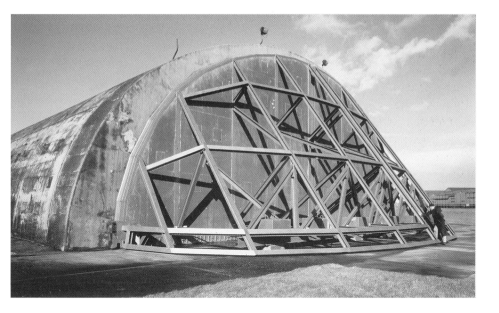

Detritus of the Cold War. One of more than 50 reinforced concrete aircraft shelters at a former US airbase.

European and North American design firms clashed in the emerging markets of East Asia, the Europeans came off worst because of their traditionally inflexible contractual arrangements and their resistance to simplification and repetition in design. Whenever North Americans competed with Europeans in Europe, they suffered in turn, through their reluctance to embrace the competition system and the tortuous learning curve imposed on them by the bureaucracies of the European Community.

At the time this unstable situation was held to be no more than a temporary imbalance. By the turn of the century at the latest, it was believed, globalization would open up enough competing markets to even out all these differences. But ten years later this still has not happened. Because all the major markets for buildings are markets for modern, fully equipped structures built to Western specifications, Western-trained architects and large Western offices retain an advantage. Half of the cost of any building comes down to the cost of producing the drawings and specifications according to which it will be constructed. Possession of capital-intensive high-tech global communications and advanced computer-aided design equipment, coupled with a preference for structural rationalization, simplification and new technology in general, confers an incalculable advantage. And because speed and

23

simplification have always been the American way – efficiency coming naturally not only to North American but to many thousands of foreign but North American-trained architects – the greater part of this advantage resides with North America. Thus globalization comes to be seen, in Asia, in South America and even in Eastern Europe, not so much as a level playing field as a form of colonization in which American and to some extent European expertise retains its hegemony.

For architects, then, throwing open the doors of the Cold War 'cold store' exposed inadequacies and opportunities in equal measure. But most importantly it brought into the open the ambiguous role of the global architect in the struggle to keep the culture of architecture and its parent art-historical value system at the pinnacle of the construction process. For in that suddenly expanded universe the increasing size of all the entities involved (including the firms of architects themselves), the accelerating shift of authority away from designer towards constructor, and the increase in the scale of developments resulting from the growing demand for large, mixed-use urban projects, all suddenly seemed to combine in a concerted attack upon the long-established idea of the designer's vision as the dominant force in the creation of buildings. Globalization brought with it an entirely different value system, a streamlined, rationalized process of building procurement run by experts in value engineering, competitive fee-bidding, regulatory harmonization, finance and a thousand other procedural and quantifiable matters – with the architect reduced to the status of a celebrity figurehead.

From the standpoint of architects with memories extending back to the good old days of the Cold War, this onslaught seemed more like marginalization than globalization. The kind of marginalization, indeed, already enshrined in the articles of the European Community, where every qualified architect enjoys the opportunity to enter a hundred competitions a week – but with a negligible chance of winning unless their office is backed by professional indemnity insurance to the value of millions of currency units, plus a proven track record with projects of similar size and cost.

Under such a regime non-celebrity architects are forced to the conclusion that any unique qualitative distinction that might once have been deemed to be present in an architectural design itself, has been discounted from the outset. In a world boasting ever more sophisticated computer-aided design equipment to aid productivity – but also bursting with nearly a million qualified architects and two million architectural students, all eager to use it – the under-resourced and un-promoted increasingly find themselves beggared in a seller's market. Selected not by ability but by auction, and employed not by patrons but by developers, construction companies and engineering firms, they take their place well below the salt, alongside their fellow sub-contractors, still claiming their historic status but knowing in their heart of hearts that it is being taken away from them because they can offer nothing exclusive or unique enough to bargain it back.[1]

Of all the threats to a once independent profession there can be none more damaging than marginalization, for it spells a progressive diminution of achievement that feeds upon itself and creates a syndrome of decline that can only end in a loss of identity. For architects to be excoriated for their arrogance, scorned and blamed personally for the dehumanization of their tower blocks and the soullessness of their new towns, is one thing. At least then they are being attacked for having abused a position of authority. But to be seen as mere *apparatchiks* who did no more than obey the orders of a cost consultant or a project manager, is something else. Then their professional status is forfeit. Once architects, as a profession, admit that they do not have exclusive responsibility for the design of buildings, but merely follow the contractor's instructions and the regulator's rules, then the engineers, surveyors, managers and businessmen of the construction industry will assume that responsibility on the spot, and having done so will redraw the chain of command of the construction industry forever.[2]

Such a thing is possible. Unlike the multinational corpora-tions that dominate the energy, transportation, chemical and food industries, the major players in the construction sector have never projected an identity that has convinced the public that they are the manufacturers of their own product in an industrial sense: that they are the makers of buildings in the way that the Ford Motor Company is a maker of cars. Where buildings are concerned, for reasons connected with the frozen ideologies perpetuated by the Cold War, the public prefers to cling to the far more implausible idea that individual architects are responsible for the hard work of designing buildings, while the construction industry merely assembles the pieces like toys, whether the result be a single-family house or an 80-storey skyscraper. This myth is still widely believed. If there is a growing atmosphere of unreality surrounding it, it must be attributed to the changes that are being wrought by the new technological realities to which we shall shortly turn. About the power of the myth itself there should be no doubt, nor any doubt about the tenacity with which it is supported by the public relations and marketing firms, 'professional' magazines and books that promote the names and achievements of famous architects. As far as these sources are concerned, the challenges of globalization, the evolution of technology towards doing more with less, the mysteries of geometry and proportion, and the politics of planning, programming and retaining control, have nothing to do with the case. The answer is genius, pure and simple. Architecture is ideas.

Because within living memory technology has always developed fastest and most dramatically in military applications, its evolution is still widely regarded as a matter of policy under the control of government. The origins of this belief extend back to the beginning of the nineteenth century, a time when wars were fought by European nations that had just begun the industrial manufacture of weapons and the mobilization of armies on a modern scale. Based on his experience at this time, a Prussian staff officer in the Napoleonic Wars, General Karl von Clausewitz (1780–1831), developed a theory about technological innovation that was to be one of the most influential of the nineteenth century. In his posthumously published *Vom Kriege (On War)* he argued that, unlike its treatment in other fields, innovation always took root in the military realm. Only later, and more slowly, did adaptations of military technologies and methods migrate into civilian life and become universally accepted. For more than a century Clausewitz's idea, summed up in his axiom 'War is the father of all things', was widely accepted as a corollary to Charles Darwin's seminal work *On the Origin of Species by Means of Natural Selection*. Quite apart from this association, Clausewitz was the first writer on technical matters to clearly state that innovation was a continuous process driven by ideas, and that the power of ideas generated within an administrative framework was greater than the power of ideology, because ideas stem from the recognition of realities rather than the adoption of beliefs.

It is not difficult today to understand why Clausewitz's thinking excited as much interest as Darwin's theory of evolution. Like the great naturalist he produced ample evidence. He showed how all the day-to-day equipment of his time had evolved from successful or unsuccessful military ideas of one kind or another. Clausewitz was the first to see that the whole of the modern world – its machines, its medicine, its transport, its communications, its town planning, its laws, its sciences, its arts and its languages – originated in a real or imagined usefulness for war.

Even today his thinking has adherents. Consider the origins of the computer, the aeroplane, the helicopter, the motor car, the microwave oven, the snorkel, the communications satellite, the 'A' range of standard paper sizes, the radio, the fax machine, braille lettering, the video game, the ball-point pen, the trench coat, field glasses and binoculars, the zip-fastener, the spread sheet, the tent . . . None of these devices was actually invented by a soldier, but not one of them would ever have evolved into the indispensible, unremarkable facts of life that they are today without military investment in their development.

As Clausewitz might have predicted, the first electrical computers were used to break enemy codes and to predict anti-aircraft fire; the first successful jet airliners were adapted from designs for bombers; the helicopter was brought to perfection for artillery-spotting; the motor car derived from the artillery tractor; the heart of the microwave oven is no more than the cavity magnetron thermionic valve developed for airborne search radar. The swimmer's snorkel started life as a device to enable submarines to recharge their batteries while submerged; the communications satellite is a civilian version of the military spy satellite; the 'A' range of paper sizes was developed to standardize the size of military maps; the development of radio was financed by the world's navies for ship-to-shore communications purposes; the earliest fax machines were used to send messages to and from the Front during the Great War; virtually all 'shoot-em-up' video games are descended from software developed for air crew weapons-training systems; the ball-point pen was developed for air crew flying at altitude; the elaborate trench coat for life in the trenches in Flanders; short binoculars were less cumbersome in action than long telescopes; the zip-fastener was adopted by air crew wearing gloves; the spread sheet derives from critical path analyses developed for operational research; the camping tent is a derivative of the oldest military transportable dwelling of all . . .

The act of bringing Clausewitz up to date by including the military introduction of digital cameras, innumerable computer systems and radars, communications satellites and infra-red imaging devices enables the contents of the Pandora's Box of military technology to be seen in a new light. It emerges as a dense layer of technological devices interposed between the soldier, sailor or airman and the natural world. It is a kind of 'technology layer', like the ozone layer that is interposed between the earth's atmosphere and the full blast of solar radiation.

Among the million interesting things found in the technology layer at the end of the Cold War was the reality engine of modern electronics – a collection of related and unrelated software and hardware that in sum added up to a targeting system for finding, magnifying, identifying and killing an enemy. An enemy whose movements could be so accurately simulated that, whether a cruise missile, an aircraft-carrier or a lone soldier hidden in open country, it or he could be dealt with in a kind of secondary reality where no real target was any longer necessary. Thus was handed from the secret laboratory to the soldier, from the soldier to the computer software marketing department, from the computer software marketing department to the consumer, a state-of-the-art mechanism for simulating and transforming reality that could transcend time and distance: a piece of equipment capable of creating reality that could become part of the normal equipment of everyday life anywhere and everywhere in the world.

In order to understand the use and importance of this new technology, we must understand the changing nature of reality in the post-Cold War world. Today we live in a part-natural, part man-made environment that is swamped by fast-evolving inventions that mate, merge, multiply, bisect and diverge, as well as regularly relegating to the scrap heap older inventions that, only a dozen years ago, seemed to be the bedrock of stability. This ceaselessly changing environment is something that we perceive with our senses. It consists of what we think is happening, what we think happened and what we think will happen next, all three randomly penetrated by irrelevant news of extraneous events from across the universe: the arrival of a space probe on a distant planet, for example, or a warning about traffic conditions on a nearby road.

The coexistence of the evidence of our own senses together with information channelled in from remote sources creates a highly complex picture that we can only understand by running simultaneous image streams in our heads, switching our attention from one stream to another according to changing priorities. As this description suggests, despite its sophistication, this process is imperfect. Like the perceptive mechanisms of all creatures, it is susceptible to tricks, gaps, errors and the relativity of perceived events, which appear different to every observer. But this fallibility is not really a fault in the system, it is a performance limitation written into the genetic code of all creatures. In the past it has helped keep species alive when otherwise they would have been exterminated by manifestly larger and faster predators. As far as human beings are concerned, it is now having another effect. With the advent of the artificial intelligence developed for military applications, this same uncertainty has travelled with us from our old primitive reliance on the unaided human senses, to the experience of a new realm of technological enhancement, and we cannot shake it off. Even scientific instruments, like an architect's CAD system, a tank commander's infra-red gunsight, an air traffic controller's radar screen or a laboratory technician's electron microscope, all of which lack human deficiencies of attention, actually invite them back when the information they provide is filtered through human perception.[3] It is only when we force ourselves to believe only those messages that we receive from the 'technology layer' that we transcend the limits of human perception. And even then we venture into areas where our perception in turn is at the mercy of the limits of our technology. For all these reasons, reality is never entirely what we expect it to be, nor is it ever exactly as we remember it.

Before the first great breakthrough in the recording of events by means of printing and photography, there were few means to manufacture or distribute aspects of reality, but it fascinated us nonetheless. With the invention of machines capable of recording and replaying it more and more accurately, our fascination has increased, so that today we record ourselves and our behaviour interminably, manufacturing a continuous mirror image of all our actions in the world. Hardly a reprehensible driving manoeuvre, sporting event or shopping trip fails to be recorded by a camera somewhere. From the beginning of photography the development of all reality-reflecting technologies has been driven by the existence of a desire to see ourselves. The more the fragments of reality captured by our recording devices are joined together into a total mosaic, the more enormous this market for reality will become. It is already so large that while the electronic media may make the news in the first place, this does not prevent the print media from finding a market for retrospective reports of it.

The replication and sale of realities took its second great leap forward with the coming of electronic communications. Print, as a descriptor of reality, called for an elaborate and time-consuming decoding skill – the art of reading. Photography required processing; film, costly equipment or an appointment at the cinema. But electronic imaging promised information direct. Transferred from wires to electromagnetic waves, it held out the prospect of transmitting sound, and later pictures, over long distances. The value assigned to this new prospect of tele-reality can be judged by the immense resources that went into developing it, even in its very early stages when the difficulties to be overcome must have seemed insuperable.

At the turn of the twentieth century Guglielmo Marconi (1874–1937), the inventor of wireless telegraphy, performed transmission and reception experiments funded by the British and foreign navies that required huge amounts of electrical energy. Before the advent of the directional aerial, to send a spark-gap signal across the Atlantic from Ireland to Nova Scotia required a steady 300Kw of electricity at 20,000 volts. In order to supply this amount of power Marconi's experimental radio station in County Galway, Ireland, with its eight transmission masts over 60 metres high, had a staff of 150 and a turf-burning power station to which fuel was delivered day and night by a special narrow-gauge railway.

Transatlantic transmissions in Morse code were not all that Marconi achieved. In the summer of 1899 he used the same sort of equipment to describe reality in a much more marketable way. With a 23-metre aerial rigged from the mast of the steamer *Flying Huntress* he reported the results of the Kingstown yacht races. His Morse signals were transmitted several miles to a 60-metre aerial on shore and then telephoned to the offices of the *Dublin Daily Express*, where they were published in the newspaper's evening edition on the same day – before the yachts themselves had even returned to harbour. The edition was a sell-out, and rightly. With this primitive equipment Marconi had not only sketched out the possibility of the sort of instantaneous electronic awareness that is now marketed in a much more developed form by radio and TV; he had glimpsed the massive market that was waiting for it.[4]

Knowing the result of a distant yacht race before the boats had returned to harbour might seem a trivial matter to us today, but it was a milestone: a fragment of the huge mosaic of reality that is nowadays put together at enormous expense by the media 24 hours a day to substantiate every eyewitness account of every interesting event within its reach, from childbirth to the outbreak of a war. This giant mosaic of reality obeys all the rules of perception that have governed human and technological records since mechanized memory first became possible. Like one of those vast, inaccurate maps of the known world pored over in the Vatican during the age of exploration and discovery – but with the added dimension of instantaneous time – the media mosaic has room for every fragment of wireless, cinema, radio and video history that was ever broadcast. Like headlands, bays and great rivers plotted on the fringes of unexplored continents, we find there such landmarks as the 1912 film footage of the suffragette Emily Davison being ridden down by the King's racehorse, the 1937 radio commentary on the burning of the Zeppelin *Hindenburg*, and the Zapruder film of the assassination of John F. Kennedy. In the construction of this gigantic mosaic, technology, in the shape of the camera, the cinema projector, radio, TV, video and multimedia, has turned possession of the map of reality from an exclusive resource of the

Powered replicas of Christopher Columbus's *Santa Maria*, *Pinta* and *Nina*, and Ferdinand Magellan's *Victoria*, built to celebrate the 500th anniversary of the European discovery of the New World.

ruling class into a mass consumption item, like electricity, gasoline or food.

One hundred years after Marconi's yacht races, electronic awareness, the field that he and other nineteenth-century pioneers like Hertz, Maxwell and Popoff created, has become the world's largest industry, responsible for 10 per cent of the Gross National Product of the world. Yet despite its acknowledged economic importance, the electronics industry still possesses no unified field theory to explain what it does. Specifically, of course, we know that the electronics industry manufactures devices based on the application of electromagnetic phenomena. These devices range from silicon wafer chips to wide-area network computer systems; recording and replaying devices for sound and image; video machines, security cameras, transmitters and receiving equipment; and clocks, watches, monitors, scanners and many, many more. But generic terms like 'communications equipment', 'electronic goods' or 'control mechanisms' barely convey an appropriate sense of an industry absorbed in the creation of a cosmic image of reality, devised and marketed in the shape of a machine version of consciousness. Nearer the truth would be an assertion that the generic product of the electronic age is technological immortality, for the production of reality cannot be far short of immortality itself. We can see this in the endless soap opera of celebrities and royals kept alive in ghostly form by magazines and newspapers. We can see it in the posthumous media careers of prominent figures from the past – pre-eminently Adolf Hitler, who appears on TV somewhere most nights, frequently in post-synchronized colour, more than 50 years after his death – or, even more eerily, the expanding afterlife of the actor John Wayne, who died in 1979 but, through digital magic, still appears walking and talking in TV commercials and in 1997 topped a Harris poll that asked Americans, 'Who is your favourite movie star?'

John Wayne survives because the networks and mechanisms of electronic information technology developed and submitted to during his lifetime captured so many aspects of his physical presence, his voice, his expressions and his behaviour that the sum of it all is now a separate machine identity, a secondary reality through which he is reborn as a digitized man. Not perhaps as himself, but as another John Wayne who can be manipulated and replayed forever.[5] In all probability the future holds out the same prospect for the late Diana, Princess of Wales.

The complex of networks and mechanisms that holds such celebrities in suspended animation is constantly evolving towards higher and higher fidelity and more and more continuous coverage, but already it constitutes a multi-faceted robotic mirror that increasingly mimics the natural processes of all human perception. Because of the professionally recorded lives of celebrities, it is now the manufacturer and vendor of electronic appliances who is the ultimate arbiter of the fidelity of our own senses of seeing and hearing, touching and understanding. And the electronics store will not close its doors until its ultimate product, a device that can simulate life itself, is to be found everywhere. By means of that product, programmed to understand and replicate everything it sees, the electronics industry will eventually gain access to the whole genetic pool of human consciousness.

Today the map of reality that is being drawn by the spectrum of products of the electronics industry already approximates to

The giant Sony Jumbotron projection television apparatus as used at EXPO'92 Seville.

a kind of immortality. It constitutes a synthetic universe that we have mistakenly taken to calling 'virtual reality', when it would be more accurate to call it 'secondary reality' – the product of all the sensory-simulating devices that we buy to blot out our own 'primary reality'. It works in somewhat the same way as the blindness of glaucoma works when it painlessly blots out sector after sector of the visual acuity of the human eye. The difference in the case of the spectrum of electronic recording devices, from video cameras to foetal heart monitors, is that their processes do not so much blind us, as change the nature of what we think we have seen. In the century since Marconi this electronic glaucoma has turned the old 'primary reality' with which our organic senses confront us into an incoherent and fragmentary pattern that we no longer believe. We no longer trust our own, or each other's, remembrance of events. Instead we attach more credence to 'secondary reality', the image captured by the video, or better still the robot security camera.

Today the market in 'secondary reality' works like the property market. If we think of the big electronics manufacturers and media groups as counterparts to nineteenth-century landlords controlling vast estates, then we can see the parallel. These electronic space owners lease or sell 'secondary realities', through wholesale distributors and retailers, to consumers, who are the end users. A columnist of *The Times,* writing in 1996, described the ceaseless reporting of the activities of the British Royal Family by the media in almost exactly these terms:

> The Royal saga is a market phenomenon that defies regulation. It is the industry's seam of gold, a product guaranteed to sell worldwide and for astonishing sums of money. Few British readers will realize the voracity of the global appetite for Royal Family stories. Magazines in a dozen languages are devoted to it. A Royal Family headline will boost street sales from Los Angeles to Lusaka, from Nice to Nagasaki. Two paragraphs will syndicate for a thousand pounds. A good picture will go for tens of thousands. . . *The Sun* increased its sale by 100,000 copies merely by printing a story about the Duchess of York.[6]

Thus the operations of TV network, newspaper, magazine and radio are all part of the same vast marketing operation that is selling leases and granting mortgages in 'secondary reality'. Mortgages of up to 100 per cent – enough reality to approximate to immortality, which is the point where time begins to stand still and reality decisively shifts from the primary mode to the secondary mode: the point where each one of us becomes for a time a media member of the Royal Family or John Wayne himself.

This transference of realities is a huge business and it operates at all levels. In addition to the not inconsiderable number of professional and amateur individuals who earn money from their knowledge of celebrities and TV and media events, there are people whose possession of a physical characteristic similar to that of a celebrity offers them a remunerative, though often temporary career. According to the executive producer of a TV talent show where such individuals often appear, 'It's essential to *sound* like a chosen star, singer, band, politician or member of the Royal Family. To look like them is the icing on the cake.' Apparently, make-up artists are on hand to transform sound-alikes into look-alikes within 45 minutes.[7]

Through the labyrinthine workings of the reality marketing mechanism, each one of us is progressively ceasing to be a *producer* of 'primary reality' and becoming instead a *consumer* of 'secondary reality'. This process is gradual and barely recognized at present, but the transformation, when it has been accomplished, will be complete. To illustrate how far the change has already progressed, it is interesting to contrast two forms of investment in reality: the old-style primary reality construction of buildings, which is denominated in space (18,000 square metres of floor space, and so on), and the new-style secondary reality production of television drama which is denominated in time (hours of programming, minutes per episode, and so on).

To build a new mid-range office building in London today (1998) costs about £680 per square metre. That is the datum cost of creating 'real estate'. The corresponding cost of 'virtual estate' is difficult to compare exactly, but television drama is an established genre that makes a good starting point. We might therefore compare the cost of putting up an office building in a conservation area with the cost of producing a TV costume drama based on a historical novel, say Jane Austen's *Pride and Prejudice*. Unlike putting up an office building on an urban site of fixed dimensions, which is a factual task, making a TV series is a fictitious activity measured in minutes of recorded reality captured on film or tape. Every hour of usable costume drama costs somewhere in the region of £1 million, or £16,000 a minute, to produce. Thus one square metre of primary reality building costs as much as two and a half seconds of secondary reality TV drama. In other words, were it possible to trade shares between space and time, between primary and secondary realities, a modern office complex of 1 million square metres could be built for the same cost as 700 hours of TV costume drama.

Fanciful though these calculations may seem, such figures do possess a supporting logic. *Pride and Prejudice* has been serialized repeatedly, most recently over only six episodes with a total of four hours of viewing time, which is equivalent to the construction of only 5,700 square metres of office floorspace. But then the production cost of the adaptation in no way represents its full earning potential. If we include repeat showings, video sales, airlines, music spin-offs and international marketing, 700 hours is a very modest figure indeed. Nor are the limits of the original novel necessarily fixed, as are the site boundaries of the building. Like the Korean War hospital drama *M*A*S*H*, a classic example of secondary reality TV, *Pride and Prejudice* too can look forward to offspring with a considerable life ahead of them.

M*A*S*H was originally a feature film about an army hospital in the Korean War which was extrapolated into a TV sitcom which was in turn stretched into an endless series of sitcoms loosely based on the same idea. But whereas the original event, the primary reality Korean War, only lasted three years, from 1950 to 1953, the secondary reality TV version enjoyed a life of fourteen years. Given intelligent marketing, *Pride and Prejudice* might well match this record, ascending to the same level of electronic immortality by means of successive series. The same long life awaits the succession of actresses who will play Jane Austen's heroines. Elizabeth Bennett, for example, the leading character in *Pride and Prejudice*, theoretically died 200 years ago. In practice she has risen from the slab several times, revived and ready to star in sequels yet unborn.

Before leaving *Pride and Prejudice* and its derivatives we can develop our original comparison between building and TV production to its logical conclusion by applying a multiplier based on the number of employees in the office building,

Manufacturing reality at the BBC. The production of an episode of the TV adaptation of *Pride and Prejudice*. It will occupy 11 million persons for 50 minutes every week.

and comparing the resultant figure with the size of the audience attracted to the TV series. This way we shall be able, even more directly, to compare the relative economic value of 'primary reality' and 'secondary reality' today, and produce some surprising results.

Assuming that our million-square-metre office complex ends up employing 10,000 *workers*, we can set that figure against the 11 million TV *viewers*, watching for 40 minutes every week, who were the consumers of the first run of the most recent TV version of *Pride and Prejudice*. This comparison shows us that not only is a million-square-metre office development equal in cost to only 700 hours of TV, but it may already be a much poorer investment. This is not because it takes more or fewer persons to build a building than to make a TV series, but because the behaviour of the *workers* in the office complex is increasingly coming to resemble the behaviour of the *viewers* 'consuming' the 700 hours of TV.

While a million-square-metre office complex might provide an *occupation* for 20,000 people for a 1,920-hour working year (a total of 38.4 million hours) at a construction cost of £677 million, the same expenditure on drama production for TV would result in 700 hours of viewing, which could *occupy* 11 million people for 7.7 billion hours at first showing alone – in other words, an equivalent period of *occupation* to 200 years of work by 10,000 people in the office complex.

The difference here is between a construction process designed to provide for *occupation* by a relatively small number of people for a long period of time, and a production process designed to *occupy* a very large number of people for a much shorter period of time. In economic terms this is a highly significant change. All existing 'secondary reality' industries, such as radio, television and the cinema and their peripheral merchandising, are based on it. The point often missed is that these are pioneering fictional entities based upon 'secondary reality'. They point the way towards massive changes in demand for, and requirements of, buildings in the future.

The rules of 'secondary reality' business – which are still being written – will one day make it unremarkable for a corporation in any field to occupy 11 million people for 40 minutes one day a week, while remaining dormant for the rest of the time. In economic terms such an enterprise would be no

The dematerialization of modern architecture into glass precedes its submergence into electronically simulated reality. A view from the upper floor of the Hongkong and Shanghai Bank headquarters, designed by Foster Associates and completed in 1986.

different to today's 'primary reality' corporation that keeps office hours and employs a staff of 50 for ten years.

TV costume drama, while very popular, is by no means the most prolific generator of 'secondary reality' business opportunities. Major sporting and music events far exceed its yield, as do unpredictable, one-off, current events of a dramatic nature. A television phenomenon contemporaneous with the first serialization of *Pride and Prejudice* in Britain, for example, was the first O. J. Simpson trial, which attracted audiences so

A publicity image circulated to encourage the emergence of new business enterprises in Hong Kong, 1986.

vast that, at peak viewing hours, it could be said to have occupied 2 million people every ten minutes worldwide. Even more remarkably, on Saturday 6 September 1997, the funeral of Diana, Princess of Wales, attracted a larger audience still. The service was held in a cathedral with a seating capacity of 1,900, but according to estimates, more than a billion people watched the event on TV worldwide. It was broadcast live to 187 countries with commentaries in 45 languages. In Britain itself 31.5 million viewers – three-quarters of the adult population – watched the ceremony on TV. In Japan, three of the five national television networks broadcast the event live. If ever proof were needed of the 'reality' of celebrity or the existence of the 'global village', or of the economic potential of both, the death and funeral of Diana, Princess of Wales, provided it.[8]

Film, TV and recording companies already operate according to irregular bursts of activity, unconventional balances of timing, and audiences rather than clientèle – all of which makes the presentation of, even the necessity for, a permanent architectural identity for them difficult if not impossible to imagine. And they are not alone. Right across the spectrum of electronic, reality-altering enterprises – from national (soon to be global) lotteries that offer 'new reality lifestyle' jackpot prizes, to the humble designing of web sites on the Internet – there are unconventional business entities coming into existence that reflect the infinite number of ways in which the sale and leasing of reality is destined to become the biggest post-industrial business of all.

Sponsorship is a relatively simple example, both ancient and modern, traditional and predictive. Yet it is a means of enterprise-funding that has become immensely complex and extensive in recent years, extending its reach from prizes and awards for poems, concerts, paintings, books and films to sporting events ranging from 'Fun-Runs' and city marathons to Olympic Games, Formula One motor racing, world chess tournaments and long-distance yacht races. Surprisingly, the last has become a particularly complex and sophisticated field of 'secondary reality' economic activity that, like TV costume drama, can stand comparison with conventional building construction and not come off worst.

When the sponsorship of sailing events first began it was a simple matter of subsidizing a skipper to fund the preparation of his boat in return for some acknowledgment of this assistance on the sails or hull of the vessel. Today that simple transaction has been bisected and multiplied so as to produce an enormous number of opportunities for what is now called 'relationship marketing'. The 1997 BT Global Challenge, for example, a round-the-world yacht race between fourteen identical boats, had not fourteen but over 200 sponsors. This was because there were at least four layers in what is called the sponsorship matrix. One company owned the idea of the race and all fourteen boats. This company then sold the title of the event to a main sponsor, in this case British Telecom, for an undisclosed sum, perhaps in the region of US$5 million. Then it went on to sell the name of each yacht for about US$650,000, and then to sell each crew-place in each boat for US$33,000, part of which was raised by the crew-member him or herself by selling their own sponsorship. In addition to this arrangement, each yacht name purchaser could 'sub-let' additional sponsorship slots on his or her boat to up to 24 smaller firms, who paid another US$350,000 to display their names. Finally, the event-owning company itself ran a stable of minor sponsors – in this case totalling 178 – who paid $25,000 for a mention in connection with the race. In total this investment produced far more than the US$1.55 million that it cost to send each boat around the world.[9]

As the examples of pioneer radio, newspaper syndication, look-alike careers, TV drama, world events and yacht-racing sponsorship show, the most architecturally relevant effects of the subversion of 'primary reality' by 'secondary reality' are to be seen not in the design and construction of so-called 'intelligent buildings' but in the emergence of unorthodox business entities operating to irregular timetables on combined global and local timescales. These are the 'reality businesses', grounded in post-Cold War electronic simulation technologies, denominated in time rather than space, and driving inexorably towards the identification of entertainment, or 'distraction', as the fictional 'occupation' that is replacing the lack of factual employment that has been brought about by automation and the growing redundancy of a work force.

While it may seem no more than a piece of sophistry to match the words 'employment' with 'occupation', and 'worker' with 'consumer', the sweeping redundancy of traditional patterns of employment, and the technological annihilation of traditional careers, suggests that some such cost-efficient transformation is already far advanced. Changing balances of power threaten the status of the factory worker, the office worker, the professional and the service industry employee alike. At the same time increasing self-employment, personal mobility, distance working and home working – along with the steady convergence of all so-called 'jobs' into clicking keyboards and watching monitors, which is already as much an activity of the unemployed as it is of those who make their living enterprising everything from currency speculation to sailing around the world against the wind – is steadily closing the gap between having an 'occupation' and being 'occupied', literally, in another world.

The reunion of the world of work and the private world is indeed a massive social event, marking the reversal of more than two centuries of separation, but it is an index of how far from the ball our eyes have wandered that so far we barely understand that it is happening. Of the shape and size, the wealth and ambition of the new economic entities that electronic realities are bringing into existence, we know little, except that they should be carefully watched and their growth measured, for they are the clients of the twenty-first century, and theirs will be the authentic architecture of the information age.

3 London's Unlucky Towers

'Today science and technique advance autonomously, without the moral control and intellectual preparation that religion and philosophy provide. Each new phase in the rapid transformation of the physical environment meets man unprepared and hence outside his full control. As a result, new scientific-technical achievements no longer address human sentiment. Consequently, they no longer assume the role of art in previous ages, when all creative manifestations of man were within popular conception.'

HEINRICH ENGEL, *The Japanese House*, 1964

On the morning of Thursday, 16 May 1968, Miss Ivy Hodge went into the kitchen of her council flat to make a pot of tea. Miss Hodge lived on the eighteenth floor of a 22-storey tower block in the East End of London. When she struck a match to light her gas cooker an explosion knocked her unconscious. The explosion also blew out two concrete walls and brought down the concrete floor above. This caused two more walls and the floor above them to fall down too. Within seconds, the accumulated weight of these detached concrete panels had caused the progressive collapse of the whole of one corner of the building. Because most of the occupants of the flats were still in their bedrooms, outside the zone of collapse, only four people were killed.

Miss Hodge's flat was in a tower block called Ronan Point, one of five on the Freemason Estate in South Canning Town. No sooner had Ronan Point been evacuated than the Labour MP for the constituency called for a public inquiry. Convened under a QC assisted by two eminent engineers, its report exculpated the designers and builders of the block and everybody else except Miss Hodge, who had allowed her gas cooker to be connected to the mains by a helpful neighbour instead of an employee of the Gas Board. In the judgement of the inquiry inspector, the defective gas installation in Miss Hodge's flat was the sole cause of the explosion, and the explosion the sole cause of the collapse. After the gas supply to all the tower blocks had been disconnected, the missing corner of Ronan Point was replaced in reinforced concrete,

Ronan Point and an adjoining tower on the Freemason Estate, photographed on 17 May 1968, the day after the partial collapse.

and three more 22-storey tower blocks of the same design were built on the estate, with additional steel reinforcement.

In the years that followed the partial collapse at Ronan Point, the event became a milestone in the politics of housing and the decline and fall of Modern architecture. In its own way it was the housing equivalent to the disasters that had wiped out Britain's lead in air travel in the previous decade. In the 1950s the debacle of the Avro Tudor, an airliner given to disappearing without trace, and the series of De Havilland Comet crashes that caused the humiliating withdrawal from service of the world's first passenger jet, had dealt British civil aviation a blow from which it never recovered. Industrialized building, another 'new technology', never recovered from Ronan Point.

Just over 60 metres tall and containing 110 flats, Ronan Point was assembled from prefabricated concrete panels. The panels were lifted into position by crane and held together by bolts, rather like a giant house of cards. The Larsen-Nielsen system was of Danish origin but the English blocks were taller than their Danish prototypes. Nonetheless Larsen-Nielsen had been in use in Denmark since 1948 and was considered a success. When Ronan Point was built the system was licensed for use by 22 contractors in twelve different countries. Only in England was it ever considered to be dangerous.[1]

45

Despite the emollient results of the public inquiry, and the overshadowing of the month of May 1968 by more famous events elsewhere, the collapse at Ronan Point was not forgotten. By a supreme irony it had taken place at the apogee of new house construction in Britain. No less than 470,000 new flats and houses had been completed in the previous year, the largest number ever recorded. But the charismatic nature of the collapse – a dawn explosion followed by the coming apart of a 200-foot concrete house of cards – lit a fuse under the whole principle of the mass production of housing. Ever since the end of the Second World War British housing policy had been about production. In the 1950s and 1960s housing 'starts' and housing 'completions' were headline news, as interest rate changes and unemployment figures are today. Ronan Point was a typical product of the post-war 'production' environment. Like all high-rise housing its construction was subsidized by central government to combat suburban sprawl. In those days, when house-building was not so much a market as a mixture of social service and heavy industry, the idea of council housing off the production line was as much a vote-getter as mortgage-subsidized investments-for-living-in were to become twenty years later.

Despite today's popular wisdom, architects were seldom directly involved in public sector high-rise system building. It was considered to be an engineering speciality, more appropriate to large contracting firms who employed their own engineers. On the other hand there was no gainsaying the fact that architects had been the first to visualize blocks of flats as soaring towers. The idea, which was eventually to surface in thousands of Ronan Point-like towers all around the world, was born at the end of the nineteenth century and all but perfected before the Second World War. An almost exact prototype of the Freemason Estate was built in 1938 at Drancy, on the outskirts of Paris, to the design of the architect Marcel Lods. There the tall towers, adjoining low blocks and unkempt 'public open space' of the 1960s British high-rise council estate were all present. The 'Cité de la Muette', as the precast concrete design at Drancy was called, was intended to be the first phase of a high-rise satellite town for 20,000 inhabitants.

Because of their responsibility for the original high-rise vision, and because 30 years ago they were immersed in public sector work to an extent that seems incredible today, the collapse at Ronan Point was a severe blow to the prestige of Britain's architects. In 1968 half the profession worked for local authorities, producing 'social architecture' of all kinds – schools, hospitals and housing. They were idealists, 'the aristocracy of the profession'. How hard these idealists took the attacks on the principle of high-rise that followed Ronan Point can be seen by the way their leading weekly magazine, *The Architects' Journal*, covered the story. There was a full account of the partial collapse in the news section the week after it occurred, but this was accompanied by an upbeat story about Ernö Goldfinger, the designer of Balfron Tower, a 26-storey Poplar high-rise, the tallest local authority tower block in England, who had volunteered to live with his wife in a flat on the top floor. 'I have made friends with all of them,' the architect was reported as saying of his fellow tenants, while his wife spoke warmly of her 'new friends' and the mothers there who 'love their flats'.

Outside professional circles, the media took a different view. Like Prince Charles's much later Hampton Court speech attacking architects, the story of the collapse at Ronan Point illuminated a sitting target. A quarter of a century after the event, journalists still sought out aged designers and promoters of tower blocks for interviews.[2] From being harbingers of a new world, the tower blocks slowly evolved into another example of the nightmarish confidence tricks Prince Charles claimed were always played on 'ordinary people' by 'experts'.[3]

In fact the 'experts', whether early-twentieth-century architectural visionaries like Sant'Elia, Bruno Taut and Le Corbusier, or later anonymous number-crunching structural engineers, were only part of the tower block story. It was the high-octane alliance of ambitious politicians, public sector administrators and big construction firms that really made it go. The names of the key figures in the 1950s' and 1960s' drive for 'output' are now all but forgotten. Individuals like 'housing reformer' Evelyn Dennington of the London County Council, architect-entrepreneur Sam Bunton and Housing Progress Officer Lewis Cross of Glasgow, council leader John Braddock of Liverpool, and council leader and later 'urban regenerator' T. Dan Smith of Newcastle-upon-Tyne between them turned the volume production of new council housing into an expression of municipal power. Tower blocks were not forced upon Britain's cities by 'supply-push' central government – Whitehall was in thrall to the idea of 'overspill', the colonizing of country towns with 'decanted' urban slum communities – rather, they were a 'demand-pull' phenomenon. Even the enabling subsidies of the 1957 Housing Act, which increased funding in proportion to building height, were the result of provincial political lobbying. The tower blocks of Glasgow, Liverpool, Birmingham, Leeds, Sheffield, Salford and Newcastle were the pet projects of local housing 'crusaders' who collared resources and actively promoted collaboration between local authorities and national 'package deal' contractors with their heavy concrete building systems.

The demise of the tower blocks was a far less top-down affair. More like a slowly increasing drip of disapproval. Two years after Ronan Point, a different kind of tower block scandal occurred. A young woman had been forced to deliver her own baby, alone on the top floor of a twenty-storey council flat. Next year there were pictures of the dynamiting of Pruitt-Igoe, an enormous high-rise public housing estate in St Louis, Missouri, which had been vandalized beyond repair. Two years afterwards the plot of a Hollywood film, *Towering Inferno*, was devoted to the idea of an architect's overweening pride coming to a catastrophic end as his mighty tower block is burned down. By the beginning of the 1980s several British tower blocks were on the danger list. Poorly maintained, taking in thousands of gallons of driving rain through their huge and porous external skins, vandalized and turned into 'sink' estates by the authorities that administered them, they became derelict hulks. Early in the 1980s the practice of demolishing them with explosives gained a grisly popularity.

Sixteen years after its partial collapse Ronan Point made its last appearance in the media. The Freemason Estate – now renamed the Kier Hardie estate – had become an even more surreal place. Cut off to the north by the nose-to-tail A13, and to the south by the railway separating it from the Royal Docks, it formed an enclave of the London Borough of Newham bounded on three sides by land belonging to the London Docklands Development Corporation. A maze of dead ends and broken bollards, the estate was a wasteland, its nine immense tower blocks joined to one another by raised concrete garage podiums and walkways as big as aircraft-carriers. Crossing this man-made plain involved giving each block a wide berth for fear of missiles thrown from above. Abrahams Point, Merritt Point, Ault Point, Dodson Point, Hume Point and so on to Ronan Point, all of them identified by vandalized name plates commemorating extinct councillors. Each of these machines for living in was tumultuously alive with people, a cacophony of loud music bounding and rebounding from one block to another. The only still and silent patches in their cliff-like façades were 'voids' – empty flats whose windows and doors were boarded up with huge sheets of plywood, the walls around them scarred black from fires.

In 1984 renewed public interest in Ronan Point was triggered not by an explosion, but by the threat of fire. An architect named Sam Webb, acting for a newly formed estate tenant's association, had examined flats in Ronan Point at the invitation of their occupants. He had discovered that some of the non-structural side walls of the tower block had bowed,

Architect Sam Webb photographed in 1984 with towers of the Freemason Estate in the background. Webb fought a twenty-year campaign to have all the towers demolished, and was ultimately successful.

49

leading to gaps in the floors between one flat and another. These gaps breached the fire integrity of each separate dwelling and threatened to turn the whole building into a firetrap.

The publicity generated by Webb's discovery proved to be the last straw for the residents of the Kier Hardie estate. Despite an independent engineer's report that declared the building safe, shortly after Webb began conducting journalists around Ronan Point the block was evacuated for fire tests. It spent the last year of its life empty, undergoing 'surgical dissection' before being completely demolished under the watchful eye of yet more consulting engineers.

After the destruction of Ronan Point, Newham Borough Council and the soon-to-be-abolished Greater London Council (GLC) jointly petitioned the government for inner-city grant money to evacuate the remaining tower blocks and demolish the garage podiums and walkways linking them. In 1985 this process began. Demolition appeared to be the next step but, after the mishandled dynamiting of Northaird Point in Hackney – a 21-storey system block, half of which survived without even a broken window – Newham thought again. Politically popular as the gesture might be, demolishing the eight surviving tower blocks would cost at least £3.5 million and remove nearly 900 dwellings from the local authority's rent roll. By 1988 a compromise plan had been worked out. The five original blocks built before the 1968 collapse would go, but the three strengthened ones built afterwards were to be refurbished for 'key workers'.

At this point a new architect arrived upon the scene. David Levitt of Levitt Bernstein, a firm that had specialized in housing work for 30 years, went ahead and designed a comprehensive redevelopment scheme for the whole estate. This featured a large number of two-storey family houses, but also the three strengthened tower blocks, with clusters of low-rise housing around their bases, 'like San Gimignano', as Levitt put it hopefully. He might have been right, but by this time housing policy had turned full circle from the 1960s, when maximum production of new dwellings was the only target. In 1988 the target was to keep as much existing housing as possible so as to avoid the cost of building new. Levitt was aware of this. In order to maximize the utility of the three salvageable tower blocks, he even proposed converting the

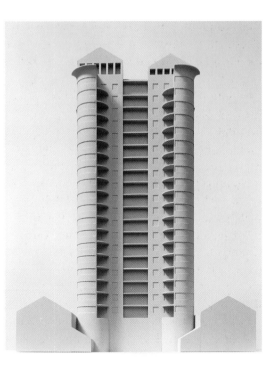

Project by David Levitt, of architects Levitt Bernstein, to save Hume Point, which stood on the edge of the Freemason Estate, near a school and a hospital, and could be adapted to house 'key workers'.

flats to 'multiple occupancy'. That way he hoped to get 330 'key worker' households into each one.

Unfortunately Levitt's scheme did not go down well with the local residents. By now, if there was one thing that the population of South Canning Town did agree about it was that it wanted to get rid of all its 1960s tower blocks once and for all. Levitt's final throw was to try to persuade the council and the residents to keep just one tower out of the original nine. Hume Point was singled out for mercy because it was the last block built, and because it stood on the edge of the estate, near a school and a hospital. Levitt's design was remarkable. He proposed to transform the concrete tower block into a 24-storey, aluminium-clad castle for teachers and nurses, with twin classical temples on its roof housing 'community facilities'. Around the base of this fairy-tale tower were to be offices and 'professional chambers'. The original tower block would be unrecognizable.

In the event this last single tower project survived for only a few months. By the end of 1989 Newham Council was negotiating not only with its own residents but with the private sector in the shape of Barratt's, the builders. Within a year all eight remaining 22-storey blocks had been demolished; dismantled down to eight storeys, then smashed to rubble with a ball and chain. Together with the remains of the access deck and walkways, their concrete panels were trucked away for crushing into hardcore to extend the runway at London City Airport. That hardcore is all that survives of the original Freemason Estate today, with the exception of a single panel joint, type H2, from Ronan Point. This was taken from the building in 1985 by the Building Research Establishment and given to the Science Museum at South Kensington. It has never been exhibited.

The golden age of the tower blocks was the age of 'housing crusaders', local politicians made important by post-war circumstances and the massive productive power placed in their hands. Tower blocks held the promise of thousands of homes built fast, and cheap – to the local authority at least – and thus apparently in the gift of politicians and political parties. They were an unprecedented fusion of production, vision and sociology: a combination of new architecture, new technology, and ideas about the durability of community, kinship and society that, for one reason or another, all failed to deliver. In the end a good part of their failure was technical – not until the 1980s was the overcladding of tall buildings in impermeable metal jackets perfected – but most of it was timing. From the outset, the occupants of local authority tower blocks were disqualified from the twenty-year race for prosperity through home ownership. In a way it was a race for which Miss Ivy Hodge's gas explosion was the starting gun.

Five years before the partial collapse at Ronan Point, an even taller tower consisting entirely of office floors had opened for business in central London, some distance to the west of the Freemason Estate, at the junction of Charing Cross Road and New Oxford Street. Hailed by *Building* magazine as 'Britain's first pop-art skyscraper', Centre Point was a 36-storey reinforced concrete tower clad in precast concrete and glass. At 116 metres, the tallest building in London, it was nearly twice as high as Ronan Point. It had been designed by a commercial architect, Richard Seifert, a man who had a reputation for getting the most out of a planning permission. Indeed the building owed its slim, elliptical shape to a very profitable deal whereby the developer made over half the original site to the London County Council for road improvements in return for a 150-year lease at a fixed rent on the remainder, and permission to apply the original plot ratio. With a very small building footprint, this meant that the office floors had to be stacked very high to reach the maximum permissible area, which was 20,000 square metres.

By the time Centre Point was opened in 1963 news of the agreement with the property company had leaked out and was already considered outrageously disadvantageous to the London County Council. But as time passed a further scandal grew. Despite a ban on new office construction in central London, which had the effect of increasing the value of all existing floor space, no tenant for Centre Point was found. The property company was alleged to be holding out for a single tenant to take the whole building, but ten years later it was still unlet. Invaded by squatters, the building had to be cleared by the police and thereafter guarded day and night. In the mid-1970s the GLC insisted on the property company letting the small number of flats in the complex. Finally, with the coming of the first Thatcher government in 1979, the Confederation of British Industries (CBI) took over the building on undisclosed terms, but occupied very few floors. Twenty-one years after the building's completion, by which time three rent revisions would normally have taken place, the GLC (inheritors of the London County Council's 150-year lease) was probably losing over £5 million every year on the deal.[4]

The story of Centre Point (or Centrepoint, as it was racily renamed in large letters after the CBI took over) is generally regarded as a tale of naive council officers being bamboozled by a cunning developer and a clever architect, but there was another dimension to the saga. In the 1960s the presence of this glistening white concrete-framed tower at the end of a shopping street, on the edge of a seedy restaurant and club district, in an area of London not well endowed with re-spectable office accommodation and miles from the mythic centre of London at the Bank of England and the Royal Exchange, somehow unbalanced the city. Its displacement effect troubled the planners. High-rise building was abuzz in the air, the child of American skyscrapers, Corbusian town planning and the bomb damage of the Second World War. It had legitimized a drastic rethink of the city's future. During the war the City of London had been particularly heavily bombed. Hesitantly in the 1950s, but with growing confidence in the 1960s, City planners had begun replanning it with wide roads, drive-in banks, sites for high-rise buildings and the construction of a high-level pedestrian walkway system designed to link every part of the square mile above traffic level.[5]

In the same year as Ronan Point partially collapsed, the architect of Centre Point was commissioned to design what, at 183 metres, would again become the tallest building in London, albeit with only one-third more office floor space than its Charing Cross Road predecessor. Plugged into an equally tiny footprint, only this time at the heart of a planned network of raised walkways, the soaring 52-storey National Westminster Bank tower in Old Broad Street was going to be a skyscraper in the right place. City planners had decided

Centre Point photographed in 1983, twenty years after completion. After remaining unoccupied for nearly as long, the building was taken over by the CBI.

that they wanted it to become the *Stadtkrone* of the City of London, the 'city crown', a title which, however little it may mean in reality, by reason of its height it still holds today.

It was a distinction that was not to be achieved easily or fast. The original client for the building, the now defunct National Provincial Bank, had wanted a boxy nine-storey building on the site, practically invisible from across the street, not a thin 52-storey skyscraper visible from twenty miles away. But planning, daylighting and plot ratio restrictions on the two-acre site made it impossible to get enough floor space this way. In the 1960s the planners of the City of London desperately wanted a Manhattan skyline and they had in mind the headquarters tower of the National Westminster Bank (successor to the National Provincial) as the tallest tower in it. The City planning department actually recommended Richard Seifert as the architect for the job. When it came to towers his was the name on everyone's lips. So in August 1968 the bank appointed him.

As he had at Centre Point, Seifert negotiated brilliantly. He was able to trade site area on the ground for floorspace in the sky as before but then he had to contend with the rights of light of surrounding buildings which made the great height of the tower inevitable. This height, in turn, became a severe engineering challenge. To conquer it within the daylighting envelope the engineers Pell, Frischmann and Partners had to accept very shallow office floor plans, a weakness that was to dog the building for the rest of its life. Meanwhile Seifert had to field objections from the Royal Fine Art Commission and the GLC. These finally led to an exhibition in the Guildhall of two schemes – two towers with the taller at 136 metres, or one tower at 183 metres – and a public opinion poll, both called for by the Secretary of State for the Environment. The vote was decisively for 183 metres, but all of this imposed delays. Even a year after construction began on site in 1971 the technicality of the expiry of planning permission almost led to the abandonment of the whole project. As it was, the building was not completed and fully operational until just before Her Majesty the Queen performed the opening ceremony in June 1981.

Late though it was, the £72 million tower was a technical marvel. Springing from deep pilings like the trunk of a tree, its office floors hanging off the central structural core and

The National Westminster Tower nearing completion. Ten years under construction, at the time of its royal opening in 1981 it was the tallest cantilevered building in the world and the *Stadtkrone* of the City of London.

resting on massive 3,000 tonne concrete cantilevers, it was for a time the tallest unbraced building in the world. Its 50 office floors, served by double-decker lifts, housed 2,500 office workers in computer-controlled air-conditioned comfort.[6] Outside the elegantly tinted windows a patent automatic screen washer system worked day and night to keep 2,000 square metres of glass cladding clean. On the roof gas turbine emergency generators were ready to maintain power supplies.

Alas, Richard Seifert's state-of-the-art bank headquarters was destined to remain a paragon for only as long as it had taken to build, and during half of that time a managerial and electronics revolution had been sweeping through the financial services industry, marginalizing the building's inadequate office floor plates with every technological advance. A year after the deregulation of the Stock Exchange in 1986 came the stock market crash of 1987, and the rapid decline of the whole commercial property market followed. Before its magnificent headquarters building was ten years old the

National Westminster Bank was already closing branches and downsizing by shedding staff. At the same time doubts about the adaptability of the tower in the face of new technology increased. The office floor plates were not only too small in plan but too close together vertically for the cabling and powerful air-conditioning systems needed to serve new electronic workstations. Beginning in 1990, the future of the building uncertain, the bank started to evacuate the tower, moving key departments out one by one to cheaper low-rise accommodation until only a skeleton staff remained.

By 1990 the City planners too had fallen out of love with skyscrapers. They had already ceased street-widening and basement parking for cars, and shunned the ambitious but incomplete network of raised walkways like the plague. Under different leadership by the mid-1980s, they had veered towards a conservation stance, advocating the refurbishment of old buildings and the retention of old façades in front of new serviced floor space. In order to reopen historic vistas they authorized the demolition of 1960s office blocks and declared conservation areas to protect the status of older buildings over 60 per cent of the area of the City.

By April 1992 the National Westminster Tower was virtually unoccupied and so many walkways had been blocked off and broken up that access from them to the tower was no longer possible, thus making nonsense of its elaborate multi-level entrances and the dedicated public open space that had been created at its foot. In that month the first big IRA City bomb, detonated outside the Baltic Exchange in Saint Mary Axe, inflicted damage on the building. But after the bomb, apart from clearing up, nothing was done and the building was left empty. The *coup de grâce* came one year later when the tower was one of 157 buildings severely damaged by a second one-tonne IRA lorry bomb exploded in Bishopsgate.

The Bishopsgate bomb was a body-blow to the City, triggering more than £1 billion in insurance claims. Fifty of the buildings damaged by the explosion remained out of operation for more than two years. In the aftermath the fate of the National Westminster Tower hung in the balance.[7] For a time demolition was on the cards but, in the summer of 1994, the bank finally decided to carry out a three-year, £40 million cladding renewal and fit-out, to designs by GMW Architects. Eighteen months later the freehold of the prestige headquarters building was put on the market at a rumoured £189 million. Bought by a German property company for an undisclosed sum, it was converted into a single- or multi-tenancy building and renamed the International Financial Centre, with 'from 10 square metres to 29,000 square metres' of office space available. Reopened in the autumn of 1997, the character of the building was considerably changed by its reconstruction. Apart from re-cabling and ducting the office floors for new information technology and air-conditioning equipment, the original tinted float glass of the tower was replaced with shatterproof laminated double glazing held in place by special rebated steel frames designed to prevent blow-out in the event of further terrorist bombings. In the same way the stainless steel air ducts running up the outside of the building were reinforced to protect them from damage. Most dramatically, access to the building itself was limited to a three-storey laminated glass and steel box running from the pavement line in Old Broad Street back to the foot of the tower. All trace of the old high-level walkways and the multi-level access designed for them was gone. The vast new glass lobby was perhaps an aesthetic improvement, but it too has a security function. It permits a thorough vetting of visitors before they reach the tower.

On the morning of 31 July 1985, prime minister Margaret Thatcher donned a hard-hat, gave a speech and mounted a mechanical digger to shift a bucket of rubble in the forecourt of London's Liverpool Street railway station on the north-eastern edge of the City. The occasion was the groundbreaking ceremony for a 140,000-square-metre office complex around a tree-planted pedestrian square designed by architects Arup Associates. This was the beginning of Broadgate, the first truly massive financial services development of the 1980s boom, and destined to be the greatest success of the decade. In her speech Mrs Thatcher told her invited audience, 'You have much to achieve in this great development, but you must always remember that it will be placed amidst the City architecture of Christopher Wren, Robert Adam and Inigo Jones.'

One of the reasons the resultant property boom exposed the shortcomings of the National Westminster Tower was because, starting with a whisper in 1984 and reaching a crescendo in the 'golden year' between the deregulation of

The NatWest Tower was so badly damaged by the April 1993 Bishopsgate blast that demolition was seriously considered. This picture shows damage to the Hongkong and Shanghai Bank in the foreground and the NatWest Tower behind.

the Stock Exchange in 1986 and the stock market crash of October 1987, the City of London came to believe that it could only keep pace with New York and Tokyo as a world financial centre if it was prepared to build a million square metres of electronic superbanks with huge securities-dealing rooms like Broadgate. Not skyscrapers but 'groundscrapers', these were to be huge nine- to eleven-storey buildings with immense floor plates interrupted by as few columns as possible and with floor-to-ceiling heights of as much as 6 metres to accommodate cabling and air-conditioning ducts.

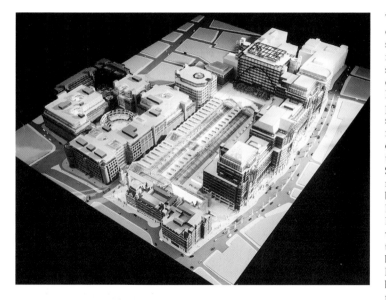

The Broadgate development started out as a modest 140,000-square-metre office development (far left). Subsequent phases included a skating rink, air rights buildings over the railway tracks at Liverpool Street Station, and massive new buildings facing Bishopsgate (right). By the time they were finished, the Broadgate buildings may have looked 'historical', but they contained more than 400,000 square metres of state-of-the-art office floorspace.

The demand for these mythological 'new age' buildings tormented the City. Confronted with the threatened loss of its tax base if such developments took root in neighbouring boroughs – a process that Broadgate itself had started by tip-toeing into Islington, but that promised to go much further, into Hackney, Tower Hamlets, Westminster and even across the river into Lambeth – the City finally broke the log-jam by announcing permission for air-rights developments over London Wall, recommending the redevelopment of 100,000 square metres on Lower Thames Street, and removing all limits on 'mole rights', developments below ground level.

These measures cleared the bureaucratic jungle for a potential 100,000 square metres of new office building in the City. The only restriction was that there should be no more high-rise architecture; the *Stadtkrone* was already there, and only contextual invisibility would be allowed. Spreading out from its original site, Broadgate soon engulfed Liverpool Street railway station and partially covered it with air-rights buildings cantilevered out over the tracks. Over the next five years the development grew from 140,000 to nearly 400,000 square metres of offices in fourteen massive buildings. At the same time the old Billingsgate Fish Market was converted into what is still the largest unused dealing floor in the City; the five-storey St Martin's le Grand post office was converted into a ten-storey bank with 40,000 square metres of high-tech banking floorspace; and the old *Daily Telegraph* newspaper building was turned into a mere façade in front of another 40,000 square metres of banking floorspace for Goldman Sachs.[8]

Because of the City's restrictive planning policies, the first London connection between immense floor plates and building high to achieve concentrated use of the existing urban infrastructure was not made in the financial district at all. Instead, not much further east of the National Westminster Tower than Centre Point was to the west of it, there emerged the greatest property gamble, and the tallest London building of the century, at Canary Wharf.

Canary Wharf was the dream of an American architect and developer named G. Ware Travelstead who visited London in the early 1980s and took the trouble to find out what the term 'enterprise zone' really meant. He travelled two miles east of the heritage-strapped heart of the City of London and found nearly 100 acres of near derelict quays and basins stretching across the neck of a dismal peninsula called the Isle of Dogs. This was the 'Canary Wharf Enterprise Zone', where a desperate LDDC was begging entrepreneurs to build anything they liked, and offering them ten years tax-free into the bargain. Travelstead could hardly believe his eyes and ears. Not only were the towers of the City so close that it seemed you could almost touch them, but just over a mile in the opposite direction was a derisory airport, but with potential for development. The LDDC could hardly believe its eyes and ears either. Until Travelstead arrived it had only been able to attract fruit juice and sandals projects, a typical one resembling nothing so much as a small fishing village in Sarawak. Travelstead thought he could do better. He proposed that he should buy the site and start the development off with three 250-metre-tall Manhattan-style office towers and a street of lower office buildings laid out in the wasteland like a giant version of a Mid western town. The first phase of his development alone would consist of no fewer than one million square metres of serviced floor space: two other phases of similar size would follow.

When the details of this monster project began to emerge in the press in 1985, most people were incredulous, particularly in the City. Mindful of the Duke of Cambridge's dictum that 'The time for change is when it can no longer be resisted', the popular view was that the scheme was probably in contravention of planning law and would be prevented from going ahead by the Department of the Environment on one pretext or another. Either that, or it would prove impossible to finance. In any case it would be easily resisted. Even if by some unimaginable freak of chance it were to be built, how would anybody get there? Surely hard-headed financiers would understand that. Why, all there was was a toytown train service that was always giving trouble: 'Three men checking the tickets and no one driving the train', as was said at the time.

Travelstead dismissed these fears. The details of his agreement with the Development Corporation were never revealed but the terms were certainly favourable. In 1984 the LDDC was desperate for serious investment and sources spoke of Travelstead's First Boston/Credit Suisse consortium getting an option on 71 acres of docks and water for a knockdown price of £30 million. Whatever the exact figures were, they were good enough for Travelstead to believe that if everybody stuck to the deal and kept his nerve, including the constructors of three landmark towers, the result would be tremendously profitable. Highways, railways and public transport, he said, would have no choice but to beat a path to his door.

So far so good. But even as Travelstead's master planners, the Chicago firm of Skidmore Owings and Merrill, moved from conceptual to detailed design, and even as the consortium successfully fielded attacks from the GLC, Greenwich Borough Council and the Royal Fine Art Commission, things upstream were moving in the opposite direction. The City had become euphoric about the prospect of the 'Big Bang', the deregulation of the Stock Exchange scheduled for October 1996 and, as a result, the hunt for 'American-sized High-Tech' office floor space was on. As rents soared in the City, cheaper neighbouring boroughs began to attract developers. Soon even building land in Docklands, once the subject of jokes, quadrupled in value to £2 million or more an acre. Before long the Travelstead, First Boston/Credit Suisse consortium found itself sitting on a site worth £150 million with an entitlement to another £900 million in grants and incentives, for which it was committed to pay a mere £30 million.

The 1985 model (a) shows the full Canary Wharf development with three towers as planned prior to the Olympia & York takeover. The 1987 model (b) shows the subsequent relocation of the towers, the foremost now in the position occupied by the only tower to be built.

For one reason or another the consortium never closed the deal. By 1987, the 'golden year', the picture had become opaque. There was a Master Building Agreement between the LDDC and the consortium, but the act of signing it was repeatedly postponed. There were rumours that the LDDC was scouring the small print of the option, trying to find a way of getting the consortium to pay more. And of course there was always the possibility that the consortium would

63

sell the whole project on to another developer. In effect this is what happened. In June 1987 Travelstead's banks, First Boston / Credit Suisse and Morgan Stanley International, withdrew from the consortium and within a month Travelstead himself had gone, his position taken by the Reichmann Brothers of Toronto, controllers of the powerful North American firm Olympia & York. Very shortly after the changeover, the Master Building Agreement was signed.

Clearly the new developer had agreed to pay more for the land, for Travelstead's much-quoted £1.5 billion cost estimate for the whole development soon turned into an O&Y estimate of £3–4 billion. At the same time O&Y appointed new architects and ordered a design review, with the aim of reducing the construction cost and shortening the contract time for the first phase of the project. It is hard to determine who came out best from this game of musical chairs, for only three months after the deal was cut, the 'golden year' ended when the world's stock exchanges crashed and the recession that was eventually to bankrupt Olympia & York began.[9]

Little realizing that they were in a race against time that they could not win, the Reichmann Brothers set a cracking pace in their efforts to complete their outpost financial centre in advance of the transport infrastructure needed to connect it to the rest of London. Having secured agreement that road tunnels would be built, the Docklands Light Railway would connect with the London Underground at Bank, and the Jubilee Line of the London Underground would be extended to Canary Wharf itself, it seemed to them that the key to the success of the development was now the buildings themselves, notably the charismatic impact of the first 257-metre tower, which was expected at that time to be the tallest in Europe.

Today Canary Wharf is still dominated by that first giant tower. At 245 metres it is slightly lower than was originally planned, and its two companions have yet to appear. Designed by the American architect Cesar Pelli (1926–), its correct name is Number One Canada Square, but to most it is still the Canary Wharf Tower. A 46-storey steel-framed structure clad in stainless steel, it is now only the third tallest occupied building in Europe (after the Frankfurt Commerzbank, designed by Foster & Partners, and the Messeturm, also in Frankfurt, designed by Helmut Jahn (1940–)), but still

A section through the Canary Wharf Tower, designed by Cesar Pelli and Associates. It was the first British building big enough to combine large floor plates with discontinuous lift shafts and sky lobbies in the American manner.

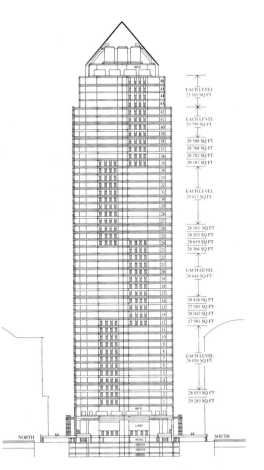

An artist's impression of how the Olympia & York Canary Wharf development would have looked after completion as London's 'alternative financial centre', published just before the failure of the development consortium.

the tallest in Britain. It has a gross lettable area of 120,000 square metres, six times more than Centre Point and four times more than the former National Westminster Tower. In addition, unlike either of these predecessors, every floor in the tower offers nearly 3,000 square metres of office floor space in a rational and efficient square shape, with floor-to-floor heights sufficient for any amount of new technology.

The construction of Number One Canada Square began in the summer of 1988. Exactly three years later, in August 1991, its first tenants moved in. Formidable achievement in fast-track construction though this was, it was not formidable enough. Within nine months of the completion of the tower, with less than 40 per cent of its state-of-the-art office floor space let, Olympia & York went into receivership. The entire world economy had been transformed by the crash of 1987 and its aftermath, and with it went the boom market for international financial services buildings. The new tower had been no more able to keep up with this transformation than had the 1,000-year-old Tower of London two miles up the river. One giveaway of the Canary Wharf Tower's inflexibility is still to be seen in the desperate attempts that were made to accelerate its completion during fitting out. The structural frame had been built with two floors 4.3 metres high to allow for 'dealing-room size' cabling and air-conditioning equipment, the lack of which had crippled the prospects of the National Westminster Tower. In the event there was no demand for these 'dealing-room' floors and these floors were completed as conventional offices. One result is that their raised floor levels are above the sill level of the windows.

In 1995 Canary Wharf returned from bankruptcy. Most of the tower was let to newspaper publishers and more than 100,000 square metres of commercial space was let in the surrounding buildings during the year. In December the Reichmann Brothers themselves returned as partners in a new investment consortium, International Property Corporation Ltd. This debt-shedding procedure has a pleasing symmetry but it should not be allowed to obscure the harsh lesson of the project's earlier financial failures. The Canary Wharf development is already on its fourth ownership in ten years and, at the time of writing, 20 per cent of the office floor space there has never been let.

When the poet William Wordsworth gazed at the City of London from Westminster Bridge on that celebrated September morning in 1802, he could scarcely have foreseen the change in meaning that its towers, domes, theatres and temples would have undergone two centuries later. St Paul's Cathedral, which in his time was almost as much an alien invasion as the Canary Wharf Tower is now, has come to exercise an almost occult power over its surroundings. Invisibly, a complicated system of vision corridors centred on the dome determines the height and bulk of any new building that threatens to intervene. In the same way, if the very houses still seem asleep, as Wordsworth said, it is only because so many are derelict, as they are in the streets around the Bank of England, where they may not be demolished, altered or replaced. What remains of Wordsworth's City – and that part of the City that was built in the century after his death – is imprisoned by preservation. It is as though 'Upon Westminster Bridge' had sealed its image for ever, while allowing its substance to leak away to fringe boroughs, to the Isle of Dogs and to rival cities on the continent.

Today there is a deadly conflict between Wordsworth's image of a sleeping City that cannot be touched, and the need for a mighty heart that will beat more strongly than ever before. The mercantile London that Wordsworth knew has vanished, and in its place has come the thin air of invisible exports worth £25 billion a year.

When the huge terrorist bomb of April 1992 devastated the Baltic Exchange, the City's conservation bodies tried to insist on its reconstruction, but the project was impossibly uneconomic. In 1994 the Baltic Exchange sold its site to Trafalgar House Property Ltd, later to become part of the Norwegian Kvaerner engineering group. Combined with two adjoining sites, this purchase created a prime 1.4-acre freehold at the centre of the City. In this unpredictable way the doors of opportunity opened for another great tower, taller than anything ever conceived before in London.

The new site had many advantages. It was untouched by the invisible rays of restriction emanating from St Paul's. It lay outside the central conservation area, and it was located within a cluster of older tall buildings, including the *Stadtkrone* itself, the former National Westminster Bank Tower. Convinced of its value, Trafalgar House Property held an architectural

competition for ideas for the Baltic Exchange site. Without exception every competitor proposed a tower. The chosen project was a streamlined 95-storey, 385-metre steel- and concrete-framed tower clad in glass designed by Foster & Partners, architects of the Frankfurt Commerzbank. The London Millennium Tower, as the project was optimistically christened (on the basis that it could be built by the year 2000), was a breathtakingly transparent-looking structure, immensely innovative in its technical design, with no central core and sky lobbies 30 floors apart, served by double-decker lifts.[10] It was also a structure that came straight to the point. This was a building that could deliver 160,000 square metres of state-of-the-art office floorspace in floor plates of 2,000 square metres, straight to the heart of the City, on the doorstep of the Bank of England. Not only that, but a public viewing gallery, restaurants, 40,000 square feet of retail space and over 70 luxury apartments. Like the great Asian towers of the 1990s, the Millennium Tower would not have consisted solely of offices. It was an elaborate mixed-use structure capable of serving a wide variety of consumers, from large financial services clients searching for 50,000 square metres of trading floor and office space, to smaller commercial tenants, apartment dwellers, shoppers, diners, visitors, tourists and staff. As a result it would have been alive seven days a week and open at all hours. Such a mix of uses, in a tower with a

The London Millennium Tower as it would have appeared from the restaurant of the Oxo Tower. The project's 385-metre height and dominance of the City skyline aroused implacable conservationist opposition. Its site was later sold on to another developer for a more modest project.

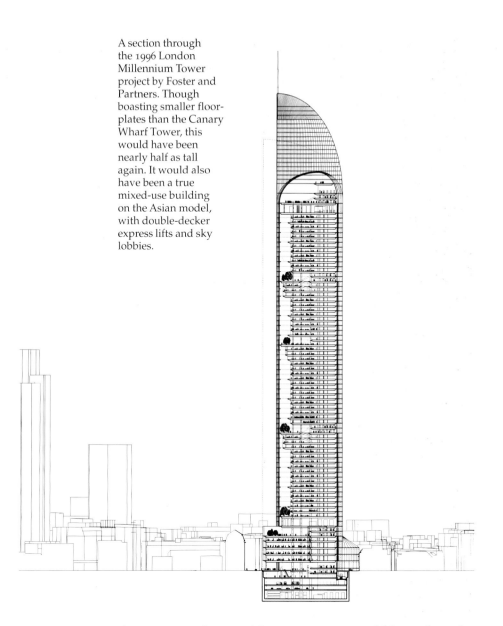

A section through the 1996 London Millennium Tower project by Foster and Partners. Though boasting smaller floor-plates than the Canary Wharf Tower, this would have been nearly half as tall again. It would also have been a true mixed-use building on the Asian model, with double-decker express lifts and sky lobbies.

daytime population of 8,000 or more, would have forged a unique relationship with the old City. Touching its historic urban tissue only at its base, the London Millennium Tower would have injected a powerful stimulant into the City's bloodstream, acting as a local resource as well as a link with the growing network of super-high towers around the world.

But it was not to be. Within months of the beginning of serious negotiations with the City planners the authorities

69

invited the developers to withdraw the scheme and have their architects propose alternative lower versions at 300 metres and 114 metres respectively. The choice of height for the lower scheme, just two metres lower than Centre Point, built 30 years before, provided an apt commentary on the relationship between towers and London. The city is not a lucky place to have high ambitions: much of the journey from Ronan Point to the London Millennium Tower has been made in reverse.

4 The Skyscraper Goes East

'The social significance of the tall building is its most important attribute. It should be a proud and soaring thing that makes a powerful appeal to the architectural imagination, but where imagination is absent the case is hopeless.'
LOUIS SULLIVAN, 1896

If London has a uniquely poor track record in the matter of tall buildings, which might in part be a matter of notoriously combative politics, poor ground conditions and a general resistance to what is seen as an alien form of building, the United States of America is quite different. From the 1870s onward America bred fervid apostles of building tall, not least the Chicago architect Louis Henry Sullivan (1856–1924), a pioneer of the Chicago school, who lived through the heroic decade at the end of the nineteenth century when the maximum height of a commercial office building in America leapt from 9 to 26 storeys. Sullivan knew from that early race to the skies that the force behind such a leap could never be entirely rational.[1] Without architectural imagination, that rush of enthusiasm impervious to logic that comes with monumental ambition and the availability of new technology, no hard-headed business person would ever build an inch higher than their competitors. Certainly the great medieval cathedral builders of Europe, the world's first high-rise designers, were driven by a religious vision, not by economics, when they erected 80 enormous cathedrals over a period of 300 years, the spire of the tallest, at Strasbourg, reaching a height of 142 metres, as tall as a 40-storey building today.

The combination word 'skyscraper', which defiantly clings to its place as the most popular descriptor of tall buildings, originated in the nineteenth century when it was the name given to the very highest sail that could be unfurled to enable a clipper ship to make its best speed. As far as can be ascertained it was first applied to buildings at the climax of the sailing-ship era, in the 1870s when the world's first commercial office block with a passenger lift, the seven-storey Equitable Life Assurance Building, opened its doors in New

York. For more than a century thereafter the story of commercial skyscraper building was to remain almost exclusively American, the physical expression of an endless battle for economic supremacy between the cities of Chicago and New York.

The importance of new technology in the heady mix of enthusiasm necessary to break the height record was evident from the beginning of the skyscraper age. It was already unreasonable to expect people to climb seven storeys when the New York Equitable was built. Without Elijah Otis's invention of the safety elevator no commercial building in daily use could have risen so high. But there were other limits to height at that time. The introduction of the iron structural frame in 1885, later succeeded by the steel frame, enabled skyscrapers to be built dramatically higher than before without their lower storeys being composed almost entirely of masonry, which would have been the case had architects gone on adding more floors to loadbearing stone or brick buildings.

By the turn of the twentieth century the typical Chicago skyscraper had advanced spectacularly. Its stonework had become cladding, hung on a steel frame over twenty storeys high, and up to 5,000 occupants were routinely provided with telephones, electric lighting and passenger elevators to move about between its floors. And this was just the beginning. Over the next three decades more new technology fuelled the architectural imagination of American skyscraper builders. Plate glass made for bigger windows, and escalators joined elevators to facilitate vertical movement. Then, most importantly for the future of tall buildings menaced by 'stack effect' natural ventilation, which swept a column of air vertically up from open windows, came the invention of 'artificial weather', as air-conditioning was originally called. This made it no longer necessary for windows high above the ground to be opened, thus avoiding serious pressure differentials inside and out. The street-level corollary was the revolving door, which kept the conditioned air inside by never actually opening.

By the end of the 1920s a combination of these new technologies made it possible for buildings over 300 metres tall to be constructed on city sites in America. All that was needed was the will to do it. That was supplied in 1930 when Walter

The New York World Trade Center nears completion in 1973. Together with the Chicago Sears Tower, this pair of towers marked the high point of American hegemony in tall building. At 412 metres the north tower remained the second tallest building in the world for twenty years.

Chrysler, the car manufacturer, took up the challenge in New York. He instructed his architect, William van Alen, to design a skyscraper taller than the Eiffel Tower which, though not a building, had at 298 metres been the world's tallest structure since 1889. The result was the 317-metre Chrysler Building, the tallest in the world. Barely twelve months after its completion it was eclipsed by Shreve, Lamb and Harmon's 379-metre Empire State Building, the most famous skyscraper of all time.[2]

By the time record-breaking skyscraper building resumed after the Second World War a lot had been learned about structural frames and weight reduction and new influences were coming into play. The designers of the 1950s rejected the external limestone cladding and innumerable separate windows of the Empire State Building in favour of pure façades of steel and glass. This was a style reduced to its simplest and most elegant form by the emigré German architect Ludwig Mies van der Rohe (1886–1969). As far back as 1919 he had designed a completely glass-clad skyscraper devoid of decoration, but neither the funds nor the technology required to build it existed in Germany at that time. It was only when the price of air-conditioning and the price of polished plate glass fell as a result of accelerated production in the 1940s, that true steel and glass skyscrapers became possible. Mies van der Rohe's own tallest building was his 151-metre Seagram Tower in New York, completed in 1958. Its thin-walled glass and bronze façades were soon replicated in cities all over America and, on a smaller scale, in Western Europe as well. A decade later the two most famous post-war Chicago skyscrapers, the 341-metre John Hancock Center of 1968, and the 439-metre, 110-storey Sears Tower of 1974 – the second of which comfortably exceeded the height of the Empire State Building – owed more to the advent of higher strength steels, computer stress analysis, advanced engineering practice and the abstemious European palette of steel and glass than they did to the legacy of the pre-war stone-clad giants.

After the 1970s, skyscraper evolution in America began to slow down. It had become clear that, given the requirements of high-tech construction and fast-track business economics, it not only required more enthusiasm than logic to justify building above 1,000 feet, but also enormous sums of money. This is so because the cost of building at such altitudes increases with the square of the height, so that a 150-storey skyscraper would cost, not one-third more than a 100-storey skyscraper, but three times as much. This formula has a strong deterrent effect on potential financiers and only a great access of architectural imagination can overcome it. The Mile High Center, designed by Frank Lloyd Wright (1867–1959), was a revolutionary 450-storey, 1,515-metre skyscraper for Chicago, designed as early as 1955, which fell victim to probable cost. This epic structure was to have been equipped with a flight deck for light aircraft, several heliports, and a battery of elevators driven by atomic power. But the resources to finance its construction and the technology to carry it out were (and still are) beyond reach.

After the Sears Tower it became clear that enterprise in the United States was wilting under the effort of building high, whatever its political, psychological or propaganda benefits. Though the 1980s brought forth a series of projects for super skyscrapers, all to be equipped with advanced information technology, computerized climate control and spectacular security systems, the next round of the Chicago versus New York contest never left the drawing board. Three proposals to push the record up to 137 storeys (530 metres) on a site overlooking Central Park in New York City at a cost of over US$1 billion were publicized but all proved unfundable. In the same way Chicago's riposte, a proposed 210-storey World Trade Center that would have reached 757 metres into the air at a cost of US$2 billion, was put on indefinite hold in 1985.

The 1980s may have ended without the construction of a single record-breaking skyscraper in the United States, but European records were set by American and European architects. Commercial buildings like Frankfurt's 250-metre Messeturm by Helmut Jahn, London's 242-metre Canary Wharf Tower by Cesar Pelli, and Foster & Partners' 259-metre Commerzbank in Frankfurt, the last at the time of writing the tallest building in Europe, represented the kind of catching-up operation that the Europeans had already achieved in the production of airliners. More significantly came the prospect of serious competition from the Far East, where a handful of fast-developing nations and city states had already begun to build high.

Dubbed 'the Asian decade' before it had even begun, the early 1990s saw a growing contrast between the troubled property markets of Europe, America and Japan, and the tremendous rate of growth of the 'Tiger' economies of Hong Kong, China, Indonesia, Malaysia, South Korea and Taiwan. Stimulated by the success of earlier commercial high-rise construction in Japan and Hong Kong, the politicians, financiers and developers of these countries seized upon the symbolic and psychological significance of possession of the world's tallest buildings, just as their American predecessors had done a century before them. The United States, the most powerful nation on earth for most of the twentieth century, had symbolized its dominance through its skyscrapers. To transfer this height record decisively to Asia was seen as a similarly symbolic act, passing the baton of economic supremacy from

The 306-metre Central Plaza building in Hong Kong. Completed in 1992, it was then the world's tallest reinforced concrete structure. It was designed by Chinese architects Dennis Lau and Ng Chun Man and structurally engineered by Ove Arup & Partners.

the declining West to the rising East in a way that the whole world would understand.

There is no better illustration of the symbolic dimension of modern Asian skyscraper building than the work of the Chinese architect C. Y. Lee (1938–), who practises principally in Taiwan. Working in the port city of Kaohsiung, Lee designed two skyscrapers in the 1990s that were of utterly unique appearance. Unlike the tallest towers in Hong Kong, which possess a cosmopolitan, if not generically American character, these buildings are authentically Chinese in their inspiration and design.

Originally commissioned in the mid-1980s as a twenty-storey office building for the Chang Ku group of companies, Lee's Grand 50 design was progressively developed to its completed height of 50 storeys and gross floor area of 83,000 square metres. During this time developments in East Asia had made it increasingly obvious that, to remain competitive, Taiwanese architects, developers and construction companies needed to establish their capacity to build so-called 'world buildings' in addition to structures of locally appropriate size. Inspired by the example of William van Alen's decorated 1931 Chrysler Building, Princeton-trained Lee resolved to have the architecture of his building dominate its engineering structure. For this reason the Grand 50 eschews the aesthetic of the glass-clad, steel-frame, geometrical American tower. Instead, with the aid of the Taiwanese structural engineer T. Y. Lin, Lee was able to produce a modern, air-conditioned, IT-equipped building that combined the formal elements of traditional Chinese architecture with the most advanced Western technology.

The Grand 50 is a steel-framed, stepped tower, clad from top to bottom in 30mm granite tiles and daylit through recessed single windows instead of glass walls. It is claimed that the building's pronounced cantilevered cornice projections and corner set-backs at levels 25, 35 and 45 not only give it a unique silhouette but also break up incipient wind vortices which might otherwise become too powerful at street level. The tower itself is capped with a large summit structure that

Rising to 222 metres, this stepped, steel-framed Kaohsiung office building, designed by Taiwanese architects C. Y. Lee & Partners, was completed in 1992. It is unique among modern high-rise buildings, both in its complex shape and its granite instead of glass cladding.

rests on giant consoles. This 'head' contains an omnidirectional observation deck and restaurant, providing unrivalled views of the city from a height of 222 metres. One of the most remarkable and little-known skyscrapers ever built, the Grand 50 is located on a site some distance from the centre of the city in an area scheduled for further private sector redevelopment. Completed in 1992, the cost of the project was US$14 million.

Before the Grand 50 was completed, Lee was already at work upon an even taller successor. This is the Tuntex and Chientai (T&C) building, an enormous 85-storey, 300,000-square-metre mixed-use skyscraper completed in 1998 in the central business district of Kaohsiung. Once again the original commission was comparatively modest, calling for a single tapering tower rising to 72 storeys, but subsequent elaboration 'stretched' the design to 95 storeys, using a unique bipod structure that supports a central tower above two legs rising from a twelve-storey plinth. Today the 368-metre central tower dominates the skyline of the city, symbolizing the increasing importance of the huge container port to Taiwan's burgeoning trade with mainland China and the rest of the Pacific region. As with the Grand 50, the task of designing and building the T&C Tower was undertaken by architect, engineer, contractor and sub-contractors in order to gain experience of super-high building construction. The chief technical innovation, apart from the two-legged tower structure, is the use of a massive five-storey, 6,000-square-metre reinforced concrete basement, with a displacement equal to the building's weight. This enables the entire building to be supported without pilings.

The basement levels beneath the building incorporate car parking for 2,000 cars, while a massive retail and entertainment complex occupies the podium from street level to level 12. Above the twelfth floor, twin twenty-storey office towers rise on either side of an immense central aperture designed to help the building to withstand typhoon wind loadings. Above level 32 a central hotel tower comprising another 60 storeys rises to 359 metres and is then topped by a three-storey observation deck and restaurant. Stability is ensured by the installation of twin-tuned mass dampers located near the top of the central tower.

Unlike the completely granite-clad Grand 50, the T&C

Still under construction at the time of writing, the enormous 300,000-square-metre T&C Tower, also in Kaohsiung, will rise to 368 metres. Designed by C. Y. Lee & Partners and engineered by T. Y. Lin, this building is a definitive mixed-use structure combining car parking, offices, retail, entertainment, and hotel floor space.

Tower is only partially clad in 30mm granite tiles from ground floor to level 12. Above here, for reasons of weight, the office and hotel floors are clad in high thermal performance tinted glass. At the base of the central aperture, above the 'shoulders' of the two office towers and topping the central hotel tower, are dramatic 'auspicious emblems' in the form of giant steel-framed flower structures. The construction cost on completion is expected to exceed US$500 million.[3]

So strong was the skyscraper vision in the East in the mid-1990s that Lee's 368-metre T&C Tower was already eclipsed in ambition before it was completed. The first Asian tower to break the quarter-century, 439-metre height record of the Chicago Sears building was the twin-towered Kuala Lumpur Petronas building in Malaysia, designed by the American architect Cesar Pelli but built by German engineers and Korean and Japanese contractors employing Bangladeshi labour. At 449 metres this too was a different kind of sky-scraper from its Chicago predecessors. A bare three storeys taller than the Sears building, but composed of two identical towers rather than one, linked at the 50th-floor level by a spectacular glazed bridge and trimmed at their twin peaks with decorative sloping roofs, the building is in many ways a throwback to the ornamental caps of the New York sky-scrapers of the 1930s. Topped out in March 1996, this structure remains the tallest building in the world at the time of writing and is the first to hold the record outside North America since the Chrysler Building eclipsed the Eiffel Tower in 1930.

It is evidence of the tremendous vitality of architecture and construction in the East in the 1990s that, towards the close of the decade, when all the South East Asian economies had

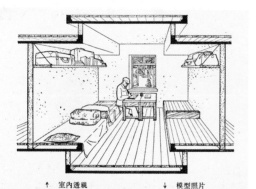

↑ 室內透視　　　↓ 模型照片

A design for low-cost dormitory housing published in 1970 at the height of the Chinese Cultural Revolution. It shows how far removed from any idea of building Western-style sky-scrapers China was at that time.

An indication of the great leap forward from dormitory housing into high-rise construction made by mainland China in the 1990s is Concord Plaza, Shanghai, a 78-storey mixed-use tower project designed by C. Y. Lee & Partners and scheduled for completion in 2002.

begun to outrun the amortization of their limited gross domestic product that sustained growth entailed, and faced severe economic difficulties in consequence, there were still a dozen contenders for the new world height title being readied in East Asia. Among them was a 540-metre project in Tokyo, a Shanghai project for a 460-metre tower, and another set to rise to 418 metres, a 500-metre-plus project for Kowloon (subsequently redesigned as two lower towers) and a project for a 606-metre competitor designed by Harry Seidler (1923–) for Melbourne, Australia. The taller Shanghai project was in the hands of the New York architects Kohn Pedersen Fox, while the Tokyo project was under development in the offices of Foster & Partners, the London-based designers of the 259-metre Commerzbank in Frankfurt. The Foster office had already worked for several years with the Japanese construction firm Obayashi on the most ambitious tall building concept of all, a 790-metre skyscraper fitted out as a vertical town for a population of up to 50,000 people intended to rise from the waters of Tokyo Bay.[4]

Widely known as the Petronas Towers are for holding the current height record, there were other elements of Malaysia's 'Vision 2020' development plan, conceived before the economic crisis, that were equally awe-inspring. In 1996 work started on 'Multimedia Super Corridor', a monster science park on a site outside Kuala Lumpur larger than the whole of Singapore, that boasted Microsoft's William Gates as a member of its technical advisory board. Unlike Singapore, Taiwan (or Hong Kong prior to reunification with China in 1997), Malaysia has land to spare. Even the Petronas Towers stand on a 40-hectare city site, half of which is a public park. At the close of the 1990s there appeared to be no way – short of Babylonian air rights developments on a scale as yet undreamed of elsewhere than in Japan – that the mere 35,700 square kilometres of Taiwan could ever host architectural projects grander than Malaysia's 'Vision 2020' development plan. Taiwan possesses a mere 10 per cent of Malaysia's sprawling 336,800 square kilometres, and Hong Kong barely one-third of one per cent.

But in all likelihood the East Asia skyscraper contest will not end with a financially exhausting battle between small countries and city states. The 336,800 square kilometres of Malaysia is as nothing compared to the 9,586,000 square kilometres of the People's Republic of China. If size really does count for everything, and if China can sustain its drive for modernization despite the flagging efforts of its Asian neighbours, the People's Republic seems certain to become the location of the most spectacular high-rise buildings of the twenty-first century.[5]

It was a paradox of the 1990s that, even as the Asia Pacific region prepared to greet the Millennium with 460- and 540-metre supertowers – with perhaps the long-awaited 790-metre giant in Tokyo Bay – the United States, the home of the skyscraper, appeared to be heading in the opposite direction. American architects were busy multi-tenanting once proud corporate high-rises in its major cities, converting old factories and shopping centres to new uses, acquiescing in the suppression of edge cities, supporting reductions in highway construction, advocating investment in public transport and calling for more high-density inner-city housing.

The extent to which America is retrenching from freeways and gaudy skyscrapers can be gauged from the domestic

A drastic departure from tall building practice, and a characteristic product of the low-profile North American and European office markets that followed the property slump of the early 1990s, this conversion of a 100,000-square-metre factory in Toronto into a discreet corporate headquarters was carried out by HOK, the largest firm of architects in the world.

workload of the largest US commercial architectural practice, in fact the largest design firm in the world, Hellmuth Obata and Kassabaum.[6] In early 1997 HOK's Los Angeles office was busy completing low-cost refits on down-market rented warehouse properties for the Disney Corporation, while HOK Houston had converted a 33-year-old, 100,000-square-metre steel-framed industrial building in Toronto into a world headquarters for the Nortel telecommunications corporation. Not to be outdone, HOK's head office in St Louis was converting a derelict factory that once made stoves for the US army, into the head office of the largest advertising agency in Kansas. Such conversions are becoming increasingly popular. At the time of writing HOK Tampa is busy converting a 100,000-square-metre 1960s shopping mall in Florida into a massive Call Center and office complex with support services and entertainment facilities. Even when corporate clients did still commission new buildings there were new problems to go with them. Publicity for HOK Dallas's new corporate headquarters for the Exxon Corporation, completed in 1996, was non-existent, the architects being bound by a client-imposed gagging order in the interests of security.

The contrast between these two modes of being is at once magical and depressing. China, the political powerhouse of the Asian decade, sees large-scale, leading-edge construction as the visual barometer of economic growth, and economic growth as proof of the correctness of the far-sighted policies pursued by its government. Examples of the latter are the 50-year 'two systems' agreement over the government of Hong Kong and the restitution of mainland property seized from the defeated supporters of General Chiang Kai Shek after the civil war that ended in 1949. This last measure alone is credited with having brought about inward investment of some US$300 billion by the end of 1996 from returning emigré Chinese.

Not surprisingly, the result of resource acquisitions on this scale has not been an outburst in China of the modest 'Green Architecture' advocated by schools of architecture in the West. Instead the whole of Asia has committed itself to full-blooded commercial gas-guzzling air-conditioned construction on a scale that thoroughly alarms even those occidentals who compete with one another to play a part in its realization. What do these Western expatriates think when they return to the United States and Europe and hear of nothing but so-called 'green buildings' dependent on the vagaries of natural ventilation, scrabbling for daylight in place of electricity, and by no means averse to the deliberate replication of the outer appearance of the buildings of the nineteenth century and before? Conversely, what do the native entrepreneurs of East Asia think when they are accused, not merely of supposed abuses of human rights, but of pandering to global warming with their simmering skyscrapers? Their answer on this latter point at least is uncompromising: they will turn off their air-conditioning when the West turns off its winter heating.

While China, Singapore, Malaysia, Indonesia and Taiwan seem destined to continue to play a large part in this drama of contrasts in the future, a question mark must now hang over the technological and financial lead held by Hong Kong. The old colonial architecture of Hong Kong's pre-war period, which was swamped by new commercial construction many years before the former British colony's reunion with main-land China, is all but lost to memory. Now the edifices of the 1980s are undergoing the same fate. The twin towers of the Bond Centre by Paul Rudolph (1918–97) have been renamed and, were it not for his role in the design of Chek Lap Kok Airport, the name of Sir Norman Foster (1935–), winner of the competition to design the celebrated Hongkong and Shanghai Bank in 1979, would be consigned to oblivion, for the bank, a mere 180 metres high, represents the only substantial rearguard action of the colonial era summed up in one symbolic structure. Characteristically it was overtaken in height within five years by the soaring 300-metre Bank of China designed by expatriate Chinese architect Ieoh Ming Pei (1917–). In the 1990s even that essentially Western building was eclipsed by the Chinese-designed, concrete-framed 374-metre Central Plaza. And until the handover of the territory in July 1997 this building too appeared to be destined for only a short hegemony, for it was awaiting usurpation by the proposed 550-metre Nina Tower in Kowloon, a very advanced project that was to have been framed in ultra high-density reinforced concrete and engineered in such a way as to provide three successive 180-metre lettable building zones, so that construction and letting could proceed in parallel. Perhaps significantly this project was discontinued shortly before the handover, as were a number of other schemes on the drawing board. The result is that there is now a body of professional opinion concerned to ensure that Hong Kong retains and develops its unique talent for unprecedented scale and complexity and does not allow its energies to be diluted by the cheaper low-density development opportunities of the now adjoining Pearl River delta urban region.

All skyscrapers, including even the despised tower blocks brought forth by public subsidy, are economic phenomena as much as they are feats of technical virtuosity. Thus the availability of investment, on the scale of the flood that became available to East Asia in the wake of the 1991 failure of the European and North American property markets, acted as a rising tide to float all boats. At the bitter end of the Western financial services property boom of the 1980s, credit left the unrewarding static markets of the Old World and floated the massive development plans of the Asia Pacific region instead. There were half a dozen countries and perhaps twenty cities there, each with a desperate desire for modern infrastructure, new architecture and new urban planning. So began the Asian decade, with skilled teams of architects, engineers, project managers, contractors and materials suppliers descending upon the region from the far corners of the developed world. Pending, unfinanceable and half-completed projects all over Europe and the USA were unceremoniously abandoned to facilitate this migration. In London they included the redevelopment scheme for London Bridge, the contentious Paternoster project (next to St Paul's Cathedral) and the improbable conversion of Battersea Power Station into a theme park. All of these were destined to remain uncompleted for years. In their place, accelerated by the power of instantaneous satellite communications and facilitated by the magic wands of governments and peoples eager for growth and consumed by the notion of modernity, the accumulated development expertise of the West descended upon Asia and the whole economic balance of the world began to change.[7]

Between 1991 and 1997 the mechanized and computerized divisions of development reshaped the natural environment of an entire ocean perimeter, much of it virtually untouched by man before. In Asia airports were created by building man-made islands of compressed landfill in the sea. Mountain tops were levelled for motorways and so much land was reclaimed from the ocean that old shorelines vanished far inland. The great birds of development left their bases in Japan, Korea and Hong Kong, and swept over the immense Chinese littoral, taking in the Philippines and Taiwan and wheeling south and east through Malaysia and Singapore, Vietnam and Indonesia, then due west to the Indian subcontinent. If their great enterprise had not faltered, these grand strategic drives would have connected the Western Pacific with the older development regions of the Persian Gulf and the American Pacific rim into a single vast enterprise zone accommodating half the population of the world within six hours' flying time of its epicentre in Hong Kong.

In Europe, when academics, commentators and politicians talk about architecture and city planning in the next century, it is obvious from the language they use that they have only just begun to see it in global terms. The idea that Hong Kong, Taipei, Shanghai, Singapore and Calcutta might be models for the high-density redevelopment of the cities of the Old World is too much of a reversal of Western history. As if to confirm this division, European development strategists employ a different rhetoric to their Asian counterparts, claiming always to be socially or aesthetically motivated. Yet time and again the soothsaying advocates of 'human scale', 'sustainability' and 'conservation', and the enthusiasts for wholesale redevelopment, appear to be calling for the same thing.

86

Where one group speaks of sensitivity, restraint, caution and the need for a tentative, revivalist, regional, site-specific sort of architecture that will disturb the historic appearance of things as little as possible, they nonetheless want it stretched as thin as cling-film around rafts of New World-sized serviced floorspace.

Largely as a result of the power of art history in the West, developers there have been bludgeoned into the belief that the existing urban environment, the one left over from history, is of incalculable value. This makes it possible for them to accept the idea that the chief requirement of their own projects is that they conform to the example laid down by the magisterial creative forces of the past. This is diametrically opposed to the view taken in Asia. Even though neither Europe nor Asia has a historic precedent for 50- to 95-storey buildings it is only the former continent that fights against them, while the latter accepts and adapts them to its own culture, producing a new hierarchy of value in the process.

Everywhere in Europe and Asia there are relics of the old and fragments of the new – as well as plans for more relics of the old and plans for more fragments of the new. But everywhere in Asia there is a mentality that can accommodate more and bigger fragments of the new, laid down with far less reference to the survival of the old. Just as the driver of a car believes that because there is petrol in the fuel tank the engine will start whenever the key is turned, so the promoters of all the grand Asian development schemes of the 1990s believed that demand for floor space would be there to enable their projects to be let when they were finished. In short, from the beginning they never lacked the 'architectural imagination' that Sullivan spoke of.

In Europe the conviction that the economy will support development is not only missing but remains highly suspect. It has been missing since the end of the 1980s property boom. During the decade that followed, Europe's cities seemed to haemorrhage jobs, population and investment, while Asia's cities seemed to multiply jobs, population and investment. The long-term outcome of this contest remains in doubt. Capital-intensive automation may keep Europe competitive for a time, but will it carry the social burden of a workless continent? In Asia, as the management guru Charles Handy has argued in *The Future of Work*, a strong family structure

makes trickle-down prosperity work. Each successful Asian business demonstrates its success by employing more workers and, as it grows, it takes more office or factory space and builds more buildings and creates more jobs. In Europe there is no longer any such growth culture. It can be argued that it died in the recessionary aftermath of the 1974 energy crisis. As a result each successful European business celebrates its success by investing in more automation, making do with fewer buildings and employing fewer people. Its very success in this sense masks a social failure that directly compromises the contribution to the economy that it makes. During the 1990s the fundamental importance of these divergent attitudes and practices came to a head in the challenge of the skyscraper.

It is often said that the Asian city is an old model, and that the Asian building boom was predicated on an anachronistic indulgence in tall buildings that was bound sooner or later to

The Ove Arup Partnership exemplifies the freemasonry of technical expertise created by the globalization of the construction professions. This frieze of 24 high-rise buildings structurally engineered by the firm worldwide includes many celebrated high-rise buildings as well as one unexecuted project, Jean Nouvel's Tour Sans Fin (centre), the tallest, which was to have been built at La Défense in Paris.

come to grief. That is the post-growth European view and perhaps the American view too. The Asian view is that the Renaissance in the East may stumble but it will not fall, because it spreads its benefits across the whole spectrum of society, from millionaire investors to parking attendants. In the East, social, economic and technical advances proceed hand in hand: in Europe and the United States they have gone their separate ways.

What then will be the fate of the skyscraper projects that still surface in Europe, where no trickle-down social benefits accrue? The continent is as technologically advanced as the Far East, and at present it can cream off the elite of the free-masonry of architects, engineers and consultants that moves between East and West without hindrance. The last may be an accident of the times and not an equalizing force that can be expected to last for ever. Nonetheless it is at present entirely possible to propose for London, Berlin or Paris a 90-storey

89

skyscraper embodying all the innovations tested or projected in the Far East – tuned mass damper to counteract sway, a downsized active structural frame to optimize floor space, ultra-high-strength concrete, a multi-speed lift system featuring out-of-shaft parking to avoid vertical movement delays, and last but not least an information-processing capability of unrivalled intelligence and communications power – and yet find no support for the project from government, city administration, commentators or public opinion. Such a building, according to today's structural and environmental engineers,[8] would be able to operate at half the energy cost and twice the thermal efficiency of a typical eight-storey office block. Yet, despite all these technical advantages combined with architectural design of the highest quality, this project will have no friends.

As the Petronas Towers, the Grand 50 and the T&C Tower already demonstrate, skyscrapers with many of these advanced features in prototype form have already been built in the Far East. Such buildings are not simply cultural symbols, or testbeds for new technologies and methods. They are conceived as vertical streets with upwards of 300,000 square metres of serviced floorspace open to a population of 15,000 people 24 hours a day. As many as twelve of their lower storeys can be given over to retail and entertainment uses; their towers can incorporate hotel rooms, restaurants and apartments, as well as many levels of large office floors. And, because of their height, all of this can be targeted on a site at the very centre of a city. The London Millennium Tower project, described in the last chapter, was an Asian-influenced design in this respect, proposed for the City of London. It could have plugged into the ample public transport infrastructure of the City like a microprocessor into a circuit board.

Why is it that old cities like London, Paris and Berlin cannot have buildings like the T&C Tower, or the Grand 50, or the London Millennium Tower? The question is not rhetorical, for there is an answer to it. Most European planners think there should be a clear division between urban and rural areas. They reason that the more the city spreads its infrastructure out, the more vehicular movements it will generate, the more intersections and interchanges, the more inefficiency, pollution and cost. This being so, their thinking should should surely lead them in the direction of higher densities and taller buildings, for they know the only logical answer to higher urban densities in existing built-up areas is to build high. For a world financial centre like London, a city that prides itself on doing business face to face, there is indeed no practical alternative. Yet, as we see from the fate of the 1996 Millennium Tower project, that was not the view the City of London took. As with the 1980s (despite its property boom), London is ending the 1990s with no new tall buildings to take advantage of the excellent public transport infrastructure of its financial district. Instead both decades ultimately reinforced the new 'edge city' at Canary Wharf, the rival financial district started up among the abandoned docks where there was no public transport infrastructure at all! This is indeed a democratic paradox, and it provides us with an answer to the question as to why skyscrapers will not be built in the City, now or in the forseeable future.

In 1964 the media philosopher Marshall McLuhan (1911–81) wrote in *Understanding Media* that part of the price we pay for our power to control our environment is the shock produced by each new level of technological innovation that we use. He said that this shock acts upon society like an anaesthetic, paralysing the executive so that it cannot prevent change from taking place. There can be no better example of this process than the *consequence* of resistance to tall buildings in the City of London.

When the project for the London Millennium Tower was unveiled, even the strongest defenders of the status quo in the City insisted that they wanted what the promoters of the tower also wanted – for the City to prosper as a world financial centre in the twenty-first century. But unlike the tower's designers and promoters, they wanted to accomplish this task within the art-historical urban value system, which assigns no value to the new, only to that which already exists or is threatened with destruction. They, the opponents of the project, did indeed want to enhance the City as a world financial centre, but they wanted to enhance it by way of conservation areas, vintage façades, protected view corridors, old churches and Listed buildings in such profusion that nothing new of economic size could be built where it was really needed.

When, against all likelihood, a site unembargoed by any of

these ancient and modern obstacles was created by a terrorist bomb and a tall building was proposed for the site cleared by its explosion, these same world financial centre enthusiasts mounted a full-scale attack upon it. A hostile media campaign began, 120 debilitating presentations were required to discuss the planning application, and the prospect of one or more public inquiries loomed if planning permission were refused and the promoters appealed. The lesson for the advocates of a tall building was clear. Pitch up against this lot, and the result will be a whittled-down compromise, or nothing at all. That is what happened to the Mies van der Rohe project for Mansion House Square ten years before,[9] and that is what would happen again.

Following McLuhan, we should look not so much at the fate of the project as at the consequence of its 'anaesthetic' rejection. Inevitably, where resistance to tall buildings triumphs, the City either declines or becomes more and more diluted by peripheral and satellite development. Over time the advantages of sites not only in neighbouring boroughs but in even more distant locations seem more attractive. Over time the boundaries that separate the City from the rest of London, and the rest of London from the rest of Europe, dissolve away. Over time what was once contained within ancient walls leaks away to Docklands, to Heathrow, to the M3/M4 corridor, and wider and wider from there. Anaesthetized by the challenge of the present – in the shape of the Millennium Tower – the rulers of the City cling to the past. As a result, the future that all of them claim to oppose – the steady drip of dilution and decentralization – advances upon them unopposed.

Perception is all. And in the matter of tall buildings we Eurocentrics can no longer pretend to see the big picture clearly. Because of this, the sentence of the court of history is that we shall write no more of the story of the skyscraper ourselves. Instead it will be written in Asia, and we shall read it with envy.

5 Over the Top with Art History

'With sorrow and tears mankind bids goodbye to its past. The past dies and its festering body is dragged around as an object of reverence. In stark decay it is propped up in seats of honour until the odour of its dissolution becomes so offensive that something must be done.'

W. E. WOODWARD, *A New American History*, 1937

Like those of the great Millennium computer fault, the ramifications of art history are hard to overestimate. As many financial calculations today depend upon notions of property value underwritten by art historians as computer calendar references once depended upon the two-digit code used by the programmers of 30 years ago. And the making good of the confusion and wastage of resources they have caused is going to take a great deal longer to sort out. However, once the shift from art history's talked-up 'Terminal 1' valuation of architectural genius begins to collapse into its opposite, the deculturalized valuation system suggested by the 'Terminal 2' interpretation of architecture, these massive repercussions will bring massive economies in their train. Then the shift involved will be enormous, comparable to the impact of photography upon art.

In place of the unique art object as the benchmark of value, it will put forward the infinitely replaceable replica of the art object, as evidence of the value of valuelessness. In place of the city as the treasure house of civilization, it will expose the city as a monstrous squanderer of resources. In place of the building as an investment, it will put forward the building as an expendable container. In place of aesthetic value it will put forward the value of access to networks that annihilate distance, presence and want. In short, the overthrow of art history will involve a revolution.

The only valuable role for theory in architecture must be the avoidance of the arbitrary and the pointless. No collection of subjective pronouncements, distinctions without differences, or differences without distinctions masquerading as theory will do. What is required is a system of logic that can be followed by different people at different times and in different

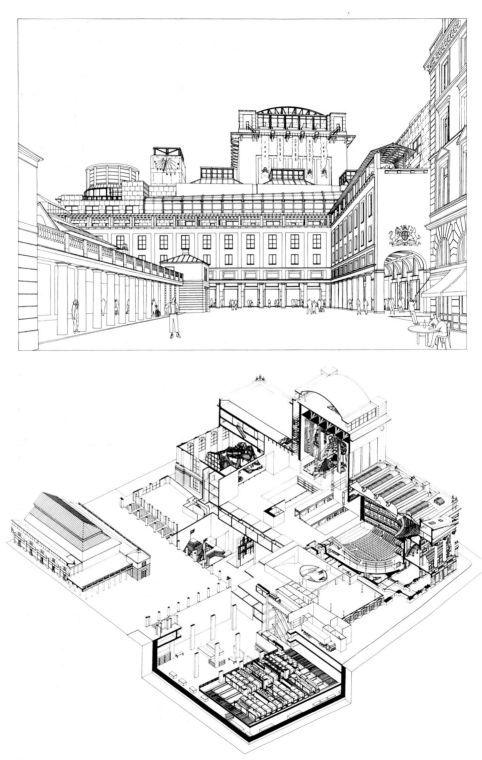

places to achieve the goal of simplicity and efficiency that transcends architecture, revealing it as a functional enclosure technology and not an occult wisdom to be wondered at. Because this goal can never be achieved by the acceptance of as many theories as there are persons who describe themselves as architects, it is necessary to subordinate all architectural theory to a value system that tracks the use value of a building, not the use value of its site, from the beginning to the end of its life, thus estimating its future value exactly as the futures market does, with commensurate penalties and rewards. Under such a regime the sentimental, aesthetic and cultural aspects of a building might be detached from its fabric by transferring them to electronic and laser-imaging techniques, video diaries and so on. Needless to say, the art-historical value system is inimical to all these measures. Instead of facilitating economy and change it *manipulates* use value by fortifying site integrity, regulating permissible uses and subsidizing obsolete methods of construction and repair.

Throughout history, but with increasing force since the multiplication of roads, canals, railways, airlines and electronic communications created the supra-national networks we possess today, there has been an alternative to the art-historical value system, a 'Terminal 2' or network theory for the valuation of buildings, and thus a second basis for calculating an appropriate allocation of resources to create and maintain them. Like working ships, whose intrinsic beauty was always considered subordinate to their usefulness as cargo-carriers, many very excellent buildings have been erected, used and demolished under this system, valued as no more than storehouses, staging posts or nodes in agricultural, defensive, transportation, manufacturing or communications systems. But while this utilitarian notion of value enjoyed conspicuous success during the nineteenth-century heyday of engineering, and again during the middle decades of the twentieth century at the time of the Modernist mutiny against the past,[1] this 'Terminal 2' approach to the life cycle of buildings has generally been confined within practical spheres. In the realm of architectural culture, the 'Terminal 1' art-historical view of the congruence of value, wealth and power has arrogated to itself the right to value public, civic and domestic architecture on the basis of infinite life. How was this ascendancy achieved?

95

The roots of the art-historical value system are lost in the mists of time, but they can be discerned in something like their present form somewhere in the object-based conception of wealth and the web of mutual obligations spun in feudal times. Art history's first modern manifestation in the Anglo-Saxon world dates from the eighteenth century when 'connoisseurship' – the impressive-sounding name that has been given to the practice of the aristocratic and wealthy of commissioning, studying, hoarding, trading and displaying expensive artefacts and valuables – began to assume real economic significance. Not only did the rise and fall of family fortunes begin to be charted by the documented accumulation or disposal of furniture, paintings, sculptures, trophies, wall hangings and other items, including houses, buildings and land, but art criticism itself started to be used as a means of influencing the value of the work of particular artists.[2]

Connoisseurship survived into the nineteenth century along with other elements of the feudal order that were to suffer increasingly from the growth of the industrial towns and the enlargement of the franchise. As the century advanced, population increase and rising urban political influence whittled away the power of the old landowning aristocracy, much as the industrial production of formerly crafted artefacts moderated their value. But connoisseurship did not suffer as a result. Skilfully the connoisseurs and their inventory-writers adapted themselves to the needs of the rising manufacturing class. Not for nothing were they described by the painter Whistler in his lectures as 'experts, sombre of mien, who frequent museums and burrow in crypts'.[3] In a century of unprecedented technical innovation and radical political thought they somehow contrived to convert an aristocratic accounting system into an academic discipline. Notwithstanding the rapid development of science and industry, and the growth of a global economy powered by steam and electricity, the new academic connoisseurs contrived not only to sustain the elitist idea of the primacy of subjective aesthetic judgement in all cultural matters, but to escape the Damoclean political question of who had the right to own what and why. Art history's ingenious answer to that one was the theory that, despite the meagre visiting rights accorded to persons other than the owner, the possession of anything that could be described as of artistic merit was not so much an exercise of personal or class privilege as a heavy responsibility, a stewardship on behalf of all non-owners and generations yet to come.

This ingenious thesis satisfied conservative and progressive thinkers in both political and economic realms, right through the turbulent early years of the twentieth century. Subliminally it buried the value system of private wealth deep in the mechanism of public ownership. After the Russian Revolution of 1917 – once the original owners had been machine-gunned in a cellar – it was adopted by the Soviet state as a basis for the continued custodianship and maintenance of all the former imperial palaces and treasures. By this means they escaped the pragmatic 'Terminal 2' solution to the housing shortage initiated elsewhere by the Bolsheviks, which was to divide the gross area of all housing in towns, cities and villages by the number of households requiring accommodation and allocate floorspace accordingly.[4]

Just as the Bolsheviks of 1917 preserved the imperial estates 'in the name of the people', so did the National Socialist regime in Germany, which came to power in 1933 and also characterized itself as revolutionary. The attitude of the first Labour governments in Britain was similarly indulgent, demonstrating that state connoisseurship was equally acceptable to Communists, Fascists and Social Democrats. In Britain, so far as the preservation of historic buildings was concerned, later Labour governments went even further, both the government of 1945–51 and that of 1964–70 enacting unprecedented conservationist legislation according to the dictates of art history. At the same time, between and after these Labour administrations, the same indulgence proved equally acceptable to Conservative governments. Furthermore, over the years, the administrators of so-called public collections in the hands of national and municipal institutions, together with charitable organizations like the National Trust and quangos like English Heritage, slowly resumed the market-driven acquisition, disposal and trading of artefacts that had been the privileged activity of the original connoisseurs two centuries before.

Looking back from the close of the twentieth century one can only wonder at the way in which art history has skilfully outflanked and eventually absorbed every philistine attack and every redistributive political measure. Every movement in Modern art, from Dadaism to the International Style in Modern architecture, no matter how aggressively directed against the art-historical establishment, has eventually succumbed to its 'treasure house' accounting system. The fate of Modern architecture, perhaps the greatest and most sustained mutiny against the tyranny of the treasure house to have taken place since the coming of connoisseurship in the eighteenth century, serves as an example of what happens to those whose overweening ambition leads them to dream of dragging the whole ramshackle structure of 'pricelessness' crashing down. We have seen in Chapter 3 how the means by which the Modern movement attempted to end the housing scarcity inherited from the nineteenth century came to be subverted. By the end of the 1980s the last surviving Modernists, like a tribe of native Americans surrounded by soldiers, sued for peace. Through the formation of a quisling[5] organization DOCOMOMO, they agreed to surrender their Modern heritage and endorse its absorption into the art-historical classification system as a style, which it never was. In return they received museum status for many Modern buildings, converting their once-proud revolutionary instruments back into monuments for the delectation of the masses alongside the palaces of the *ancien régime.* Thus was the grand artistic mutiny of Modernism finally brought to heel. As the great Modern architect Berthold Lubetkin (1901-90) confessed, near the end of his life: 'I abandoned architecture because it had lost its line. It was the harbinger of a better world and it ended up like miniskirts.'[6]

Art history, as Roger Scruton has pointed out,[7] is neither truly the history of art, nor truly the history of art criticism. It is a combination of a very selective aspect of history with a very subjective technique of criticism. Because the first of these must necessarily be incomplete, and the second cannot be disproved by rational argument (*de gustibus non disputandum*), art history, like the bumble bee, ought not to be possible. But it is, and like the bumble bee it survives and thrives because its impossibility is never conclusively established. Like asymptotic lines, the missiles hurled by the Modern Movement at the relativistic history of precious things never actually met their target. Art history may seem a huge distended barrage balloon, so swollen with fakes and replicas that its envelope is ready to burst, but nobody can shoot it down. It survives, laughable, unsubstantiated, ridiculous, out of date, but, like some corrupt dictatorship, still in control.

Scruton admits there is a kind of trickery at work here. He wonders at the pea and thimble tricks by which art history underwrites its own hypotheses by way of the idea of the *Zeitgeist*, a philosophical convenience that posits a connection between all the events and opinions of an epoch, but can never explain it. As far as art history is concerned things happen in an era and that makes them interdependent. Thus we reach such self-authenticating tautologies as the idea that Georgian furniture is typical of the Georgian age, while Victorian furniture is more characteristic of the Victorian age. Because all eras are integral, art history makes little or no use of cause and effect. A question will pass for an effect, a personality for a cause. For example, 'Where else but in what is now Italy could the Renaissance have begun?' or, 'Whistler destroyed the popular confidence in contemporaneous art'.[8] Nor is any but the most respectful attempt made to place any era above another. As far as art and architecture are concerned, paintings and buildings from time past become even more self-referential and secure in their own security (as we might put it) when they fall into the hands of the art-historical establishment than they were when perilously afloat upon the currents of their own time. Hence the 'saturated' historical detailing that is applied to buildings that are 'restored',[9] coupled with the insistence on renewing inadequate original materials for reasons of authenticity – like the softwood window frames that blighted local authority tower blocks in the 1960s and are even now deemed worthy of preservation for historic reasons.

If the conquest of Modern architecture was the most resounding art-historical victory of the twentieth century, the high-water mark of the discipline itself occurs when its tentacles reach forward in time to overpower the judgement of posterity, as well as that of present generations. The operative axiom here was given voice by Sir Jocelyn Stevens, chairman of English Heritage, when he advised an audience of architects at a dinner in 1996 that 'The people who take care of the past are the right people to take care of the future.'[10]

In recent years they have made great strides towards achieving this goal. Eager as ever to place their own construction upon the activities of the most powerful economic forces of the epoch, the most far-sighted members of the Heritage establishment have stealthily adapted their product better to serve inanimate ends and artificial intelligences. Archaeologists now use state-of-the-art 'ground radar' developed by oil companies for exploration. The National Monuments Record has become a commercial image bank with 6.5 million photographic negatives of 400,000 Listed or demolished buildings and archaeological sites – and it went on the Internet in 1995. English Heritage too looks far ahead. Hadrian's Wall, one of its 'properties', is now a revenue-producing tourist attraction subject to a management plan agreed by 100 landowners that does not expire until 2025. Even more like science fiction has been the undeclared change of use of St Paul's Cathedral, which is now a major element in the planning system of central London. Ever since the abolition of the GLC in 1986 there has been no statutory height limit on buildings in the city. Instead a complicated system of 'vision corridors' converging on the dome of St Paul's has been developed to provide topographical height and width limits for any new building that might threaten to impinge on a view of the cathedral.

St Pancras Chambers, formerly the Midland Grand Hotel. A Grade I Listed building, this ornate structure by Sir George Gilbert Scott exemplifies the 'Terminal 1' art-historical architecture that dominates the value system of the city. It masks the remarkable 'Terminal 2' wrought-iron and glass train shed by the engineer William Barlow, which was, on completion in 1867, the longest-span building in the world.

Thus the 'use' of an early eighteenth-century cathedral now includes the control of 21st-century development.

However the most remarkable art-historical success in subborning the future has been achieved at the level of individual buildings themselves with the aid of 'Stealth Architecture' – the retention or replication of historic façades on otherwise new buildings. The exteriors of these structures reveal no hint of what goes on inside them. They are buildings that, on the outside, could pass muster in a TV dramatization of a Jane Austen novel, but internally are entirely Modern, packed with as much electronic equipment as an air traffic control tower. Such buildings have also become popular in the United States, where they are called 'filmable façades'. They are not only an art-historical but a post-Modern phenomenon and their importance is discussed at greater length in Chapter 8 below. Suffice it to say that 'stealth buildings' with 'filmable façadès' are a crucial product of the pre-terminal age – perhaps the last combination of 'Terminal 1' and 'Terminal 2' value systems in one schizophrenic structure, before the two separate, once and for all.

An eight-storey steel frame assembled inside a former airship shed at Cardington in Bedfordshire, now used by the Building Research Establishment. Intended for vibration, fire and explosion tests, it exemplifies the deculturalized simplicity of all 'Terminal 2' architecture.

The comparison made above between art history and a corrupt dictatorship is valid in other ways too. For just as the secret, undemocratic politics of the totalitarian state are shot through with corruption, so are the shibboleths of art history plagued by quackery and fraud. The difference is that the parade of historical artefacts that fills every museum and art gallery is knowingly corrupted by fakes, misattributions and errors that come to light with monotonous regularity. Little or no effort is made to hide or eradicate these living false-hoods, for if it were, the whole ramshackle structure of the art-historical value system would come crashing down about the heads of its practitioners, revealing them for what they are, collaborators in the crimes of inauthenticity.

The painter Eric Hebborn, who died in 1996, may have been the most prolific art forger of the twentieth century, but he was by no means alone. Rather he represented the tip of an iceberg of forgery in the art world, nine-tenths of which remains undetected – or at any rate unexposed – to this day. Hebborn's distinguished contemporaries include Tom Keating, who forged Samuel Palmers; Elmyr de Hory, who specialized in Impressionists; van Meegeren, who painted better Vermeers than Vermeer; and Charles Mount, who forged numerous watercolours by John Singer Sargent. But to become inter-ested in this cast of swashbuckling forgers is to fall into the trap of art history itself and the whole vertiginous realm of creative relativism.[11] Sometimes it is merely enough to moni-tor the steady stream of press stories that allege this or that masterpiece to be a forgery, to have been executed by appren-tices, to be a duplicate, a trick and so on.[12]

The important thing about fakery in the arts is the indus-trial scale on which it is carried out and its pervasiveness in all fields. For if the art market is awash with false Old Masters and dubious van Goghs, so are the parallel worlds of litera-ture, antiques, music, government and architecture bursting with evidence of fraud and deception. In order to avoid theft or damage, some 'valuable' sculptures and paintings in govern-ment and diplomatic buildings are already copies of originals hidden away in vaults or museums. In the same way huge numbers of entries for creative competitions are plagiarized or misrepresented. In pursuit of literary prizes male authors imitate women, and women men. In Australia white women write what purport to be aboriginal autobiographies and are praised for their verisimilitude. Even the very young are involved. In July 1997 it was revealed that the thirteen-year-old winner of a so-called 'National Rainforest Poetry Competition' entered by 90,000 British schoolchildren had in fact copied out a poem by Brian Patten called 'The Newcomer' and submitted it, under its original title, using her own name. Instead of being angry, Patten himself commented, 'I am happy that she found the poem of enough interest to draw attention to the issues.'[13]

The world of antique furniture offers other examples. In 1996 former antique dealer Jonathan Gash, the creator of *Lovejoy*, the TV series about a roguish antique dealer, went on record as calculating that between 1700 and 1900, a period that comfortably encompasses the entire Georgian era, only about 170,000 households in Britain could have afforded furniture of the kind that antique dealers sell as 'Georgian' today. Yet the British antique trade presently *exports* more than 170,000 'Georgian' pieces every year, at prices ranging from £5,000 to £250,000 per piece. According to this calculation a large proportion of all so-called Georgian furniture must be fake.

Music too is rent by plagiarism and misattribution. As long ago as 1935 the celebrated violinist Fritz Kreisler admitted to a journalist that for 30 years he had been inserting pieces of his own composition into recitals of the works of seventeenth- and eighteenth-century composers. Kreisler came under attack, but he was unrepentant. If his listeners could not distinguish between the pieces he played and genuine baroque music, he argued, why should it matter whether they were forged or not?

Like paintings, books, antique furniture and old music, so-called historic buildings are frequently a great deal less than they seem, not least because the heritage industry now takes an interest in properties far less exalted than the grand palaces, castles and country houses about which it first expressed concern. A characteristic case that attracted much publicity involved a house purchased by a British member of parliament in 1992. The then Conservative member for Billericay in Kent, Teresa Gorman, and her husband, had bought a derelict house in Essex for £170,000. Called Old Hall Farm, the building was composed of sixteenth-, eighteenth-, nineteenth- and twentieth-century elements randomly accumulated over time, as was the way before the passage of legislation designed to stamp out architectural miscegenation. By 1992 the Gormans' ruin of a random house was protected by the full majesty of the law. It had been Listed Grade II under the 1968 Town and Country Planning Act, which protected it against any unauthorized alteration that might 'affect its quality as a building of architectural or historic importance'. In short, despite being derelict when its new owners bought it, Old Hall Farm was considered by the authorities to be of art-historical value. It was one of nearly 600,000 dwellings in the United Kingdom that are held by conservationists to be 'All that is left in this country of fine, original buildings'.[14]

Oblivious to the implications of this change in its status, Mrs Gorman proceeded to restore her derelict house to a habitable state as that term is popularly understood in the late twentieth century. At a cost of £230,000 her builder removed original open fireplaces, added an entrance porch, inserted insulation, installed central heating and Upvc double-glazed windows, removed a superfluous eighteenth-century brick façade and generally improved the property. Part of this programme of work involved making the exterior of the house look somewhat older (to untutored eyes) than it really was, because the newly added porch was of 'period' rather than 'historic' design. In the same way false timber beams and previously non-existent rendered panels were inauthentically added.

To Mrs Gorman's surprise the local authority planning department responsible for the part of Essex where the house was situated took strong exception to these alterations and improvements. She and her husband, refusing to reinstate the original work, were taken to court and accused of over 500 infringements of the 1968 Act. The case dragged on for two years and by the time it was finally adjudicated in 1996 the planning department had reduced its list of material infringements to 29. Nonetheless Mrs Gorman and her husband were found guilty and fined £3,000 each, plus £4,000 court costs and unspecified legal costs.

This was a high-profile case but not untypical. The fact that the house was derelict before purchase and had then been brought into beneficial use was not considered to be important. The point was that the Gormans had altered a Listed building in such a way as 'to affect its quality as a building of architectural or historic importance'.

The story of Old Hall Farm, like the Kreisler episode, Jonathan Gash's furniture calculations and the bizarre careers of Eric Hebborn and his fellow forgers, all have their analogues in architecture today. A modern building may be no more than a big piece of industrial design, 'like an enormous typewriter', as Robert Venturi once put it, but its unique combination of industrial components is still considered to be intellectual property, like a piece of music or a painting. Why this should be so is not clear. Getting a building built is not at all like writing a book or painting a picture. It is more like winning an election. Of all the thousands of individuals directly or indirectly involved in the production of buildings only one – the architect – is supposed to be trying to create something original. Nonetheless the rules of individual genius apply and buildings are routinely treated as though they are works of art that can be acquired by the state or one of its public or private institutions, and thereafter held in stewardship for the population to pay to admire. The consequence is a situation in which buildings are forced to become monuments instead of instruments and, like old persons in hospital, are not allowed to die but are kept alive, propped up, bedridden and insentient, in the toils of the monstrous industry of heritage.

This indeed has been the fate of St Paul's Cathedral, upon whose dome the sun will rise this morning as it has done every morning for nearly 300 years. It has also been the fate of Battersea Power Station, a ghastly hulk awaiting 'restoration' these last fifteen years. The two buildings are separated by purpose and age, but they are also linked, and not solely by the rays of the sun. Like Longleat House, the Royal William Dockyard in Plymouth, many remote former coastal artillery emplacements, Wigan Pier, many old telephone boxes, Salisbury Cathedral, the Runcorn–Widnes road bridge, some prefabs in south London, nice country cottages in Somerset, the Cabinet War Rooms and 600,000 other buildings, they are either Listed or under consideration for Listing by the Department of the Environment.

'Listing' is the final solution of the art-historical problem. It is a form of legal preservation that brings together an impossible collection of opposites. Today it threatens to 'save', not just the 61 cathedrals, the hundreds of castles and the thousands of 'treasure houses' of Britain, but workaday office buildings, shops, factories and houses that have in the past been erected, demolished and replaced in pursuit of enterprise, employment and profit: the very circuit boards, in fact, of the national economy. Every year, if the Listing enthusiasts have their way, the expendable status of many of these workaday buildings will change. Like St Paul's Cathedral, Battersea Power Station and Millbank Tower, all of which are already Listed, they will confront one another, unalterable, until Hell freezes over.

In the words of English Heritage, the art-historical quango concerned with the harvesting and marketing of historic buildings and other artefacts, the purpose of Listing a building is to preserve its character, to prevent thoughtless demolition and inappropriate alteration, to investigate new uses to which it might be put, and to consider ways of meeting its owner's requirements. Described in this way, the whole business of being Listed sounds like going to the marriage guidance counsellor, but there is a difference. If your marriage is falling apart, Relate will advise you on disposing of the pieces with the minimum inconvenience. The Listing people are made of sterner stuff. They will not put up with any wingeing about 'irretrievable breakdown' where buildings are concerned. Marriages, families, religious beliefs and venerable institutions may be falling off the social structure like tiles off an old roof, but the Listing people stand firm. Their awesome piles of stone, brick and timber (and increasingly steel, glass and aluminium too) have become our new moral guardians: monoliths that remind us sternly of what we used to be. Getting unmarried is one thing. Try knocking down a Listed building and they will lock you up.

How Listed buildings came to assume this Praetorian status is hard to explain. Listing itself dates from the aftermath of the 1939–45 war, that orgy of aerial demolition that ended with a bomb that could take out whole cities at one go. The irony should not be lost on us. It was during the spasm of guilt that followed this *auto-da-fé* of destruction that the idea of 'Listing' buildings was born. Thanks to the fact that between 1914 and 1950 Britain was at war for the equivalent of one day out of every three and a half, neglect coupled with war damage and social upheaval had created a built environment in Britain as unappetizing as the background activities in a Hogarth print. So in 1947 the new Labour government resolved to safeguard important historic buildings by decree.

At first Listing proceeded at a modest pace. The closing date for protection was set at 1840 (100 years before the *blitzkrieg* war) and cathedrals, palaces, castles and country houses of indisputable architectural interest made up the bulk of the 120,000 buildings registered by the mid-1970s. Up to then national economic development through industry and commerce, and the care of historic buildings, were treated as two different things. The first was to do with UK plc's trading performance, and the second with civic pride. It was only after the massive oil-price increases, the savage inflation and the three-day week of the 1970s that the two suddenly changed places. Britain's heritage of old buildings and artefacts became the nuts and bolts of its economy, while the country's trading performance became little more than a propaganda stunt. The result was the sudden adoption of the upper tier of Listed buildings as the nucleus of the new international tourist industry, with consequences for the deterioration of urban life that are outlined in a later chapter.

One of the first creations of the new tourist industry was the Accelerated Listing Programme of the early 1980s. Under this edict the date for Listing eligibility was extended from 1840 to 1914, then to 1939, and then subjected to a '30-year rule'. As a result there were soon well over half a million Listed buildings, most of them of little more than scenic value, and hundreds of thousands more that were protected because they were in places that had been declared conservation areas, of which there were soon 8,800 the length and breadth of the country. The heritage industry now employed thousands. It involved not only English Heritage but the Department of the Environment, the Department of National Heritage (since renamed the Department for Culture, Media and Sport), the National Monuments Record and a number of other charities, advisory bodies and conservation pressure groups. The Listing of buildings had become a massive, multi-tiered public and private bureaucratic process, awash with grants and sponsorship deals and totally committed to the idea of a post-industrial, tourist-driven economy of old buildings.

Like the booming housing market, the Listing trade turned

a pretty penny during the 1980s, but at the beginning of the 1990s it nearly went into receivership. With the coming of the recession, tourist earnings plunged into deficit, and specialist maintenance costs for ancient structures went through the roof. There were other warning signs. By 1993 some 30,000 Listed buildings were classified as 'at risk' – meaning that they were derelict and no beneficial use could be found for them. Priceless, of course, but worthless too.

By 1995 Listing faced what looked like a terminal crisis. Logic decreed that the great book of Lists should be closed for a century or so. But neither the heritage industry nor the art-historical establishment that provided the legends to accompany the preservation cover stories got where they are today by being logical. If the past was exhausted, it had an alternative. There was still the present. At the beginning of 1995 English Heritage had plans to List 130 post-war buildings, the youngest a bare twenty years old. The buildings were no longer great ecclesiastical or public works like Coventry Cathedral or the Royal Festival Hall – long since Listed Grade I like St Paul's Cathedral – but a motley collection of obsolete office buildings and such minor industrial masterpieces as a Dagenham works canteen and a signal box in Barnes.

Perhaps with an inkling of what was to come, English Heritage whittled its 1995 list down to 40 before submitting it, but, even so, the financially responsible side of government brainpower finally rebelled. The then Heritage Secretary declared a public consultation period on the Listing process for the first time, inviting comments from the person in the street on whether the proposed post-war buildings should be Listed or not. Within six months the 'debate' was over and the decisions had been made: with very few exceptions all the proposed buildings were Listed. So powerful had the heritage lobby proved that, even after five years of recession, and despite the prospect of planning blight in business districts and industrial estates as well as old town centres, it got its way again. The corrupt dictatorship of art history had taken control of the future, the present and the past.

Today old buildings are instinctively protected. We see in them a continuation of the certainties of the past. We believe that when we demolish old buildings the past is destroyed with them. We fear that in their absence a vertiginous instability will reign. Nothing will be predictable.

Such fears are unrealistic but they are not unreal. The chroniclers of the terror bombings of the Second World War recount the bewilderment, the disorientation and the repeated irrelevant behaviours of those whose dwellings and neighbourhoods were literally blown away. Contemporary urban redevelopment does not involve such trauma, but it deals with the same ingredients. Our own experience tells us that the built environment is a kind of artificial horizon, a guarantee of level flight, of normal life.

For this reason we do not wish to demolish, redevelop, alter or revise the use of our historic buildings. Quite the reverse. All European cities, even those severely disfigured in the Second World War, retain part of their ancient street patterns. Some boast buildings from the fourteenth and fifteenth centuries and before. The largest and most numerous artefacts of history that we possess are old buildings. We protect them at the cost of the distinction between town and country that has been lost in the last 50 years.

In the last half century millions of square metres of housing, offices, light industry, warehousing and distribution centre floorspace has been constructed outside the old boundaries of our towns and cities. Hundreds of thousands of out-of-town

The London house of the artist Edward Linley Sambourne (1844–1910), with its vast accumulation of furniture, decoration and memorabilia, exemplifies the art-historical treasure house mentality.

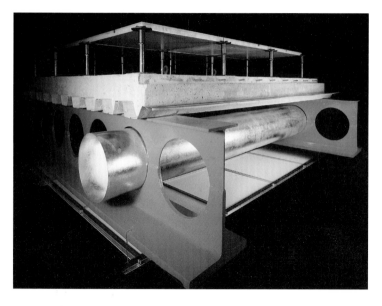

A sample of what is meant by serviced floor space, from raised floor to suspended ceiling. With variations, this is the basic unit of commercial urban development today.

commercial complexes have been built on motorway networks disconnected from the old urban framework. In England nearly 100 out-of-town shopping centres have been built since 1980, half of them offering more than 50,000 square metres under cover. Ten of them are connected to the orbital motorway ringing London.

The antecedents of these structures reach back into history. On the thesis side their roots stretch back to the architecture of pre-industrial, pre-electronic buildings, hand-crafted into a kind of usefulness again and again. On the antithesis side they can be traced through the architecture of industrial, electronic 'Big Sheds', styleless, historyless, cultureless, back to the unattributed warehouses, granaries and barns of prehistory. And it is these last that are the true progenitors of the 'Terminal 2' buildings discussed in Chapter 9. Their chief characteristic in common is that they were invariably built outside historic towns and cities. They have much to teach us, for they have never bowed to the art-historical convention of innumerable professors, students, graduates and enthusiasts, that buildings exist to please the eye or magnify the importance of their individual or corporate owners. These structures do not exist, as did the mausoleums of the past, to perpetuate the corporate or individual influence once vested in those who caused them to be built.

Today, whatever respect that was once commanded by a

specific bloodline, concentration of wealth or political dynasty can no longer be transferred to a building as was possible in the past. History has become liability, not merely in the sense that 'stylistically correct' repairs to historic buildings are notoriously expensive, but also in the message that old buildings send to those who must deal with the organizations that occupy and use them. Recent examples include such venerable institutions as the insurance brokers Lloyds of London, and the allegedly prestigious Barings merchant bank. Founded in the seventeenth century and still administered by staff wearing a Dickensian garb of frock coats and riding boots, Lloyds deliberately repackaged itself in a radically new building in the late 1970s, but was almost wiped out by a run of adverse trading within five years of the building's completion. In the end the new building made no difference, unless it made the crisis worse. The somewhat younger Barings, after 200 years of profitable trading, collapsed overnight because its directors were baffled by the new technology of electronic currency dealing and had failed to control irresponsible members of staff who didn't understand that it required almost limitless reserves. In the end the debt-ridden remains of the bank were sold for one pound to an overseas competitor. As for its reassuringly columniated head office building, once the Barings brass plate had been removed from its entrance, the glory of 200 years vanished with it.

However we try to think of them as national treasures, imbued with certain qualities inherited from certain owners or associated with certain events, important buildings, Listed buildings, always let us down. They do not care. They have no feelings. They have no compunction about having their identity changed, no loyalty to their previous owners. So what if a nineteenth-century fish market in London becomes the city's largest dealing room? So what if Adolf Hitler's command bunker in the former East Prussia becomes a Polish nightclub? So what if a twelfth-century monastery in France becomes a computer software house, or an American shopping centre an office park? The real importance, the real value of all these structures lies in their use. And the only constant in their use is their role as terminals for the great suppliers of information, energy and nutrients that sustain life in the modern world.

6 From Modernism to Postmodernism

'Looking straight down, all that I see is the bric-a-brac of another age exhibited under a perfect lens. I am leaning over the glass case of a museum.'

ANTOINE DE SAINT EXUPÉRY, *Pilote de Guerre*, 1942

Any attempt to recount the steps by which architecture reached its terminal condition at the end of the twentieth century is bound to be problematic. From the outset the selection of evidence will be subjective. In the same way – in what is already called the Asian decade – the bias will be seen as Eurocentric, and probably increasingly so with the passage of time. In a twenty-first century of instantaneous global communications and worldwide architectural practice such parochialism will appear at the very least quaint, the only excuse being the one offered by history itself: that for more than three-quarters of our century the world of architecture was dominated by Europe and America, but it is no longer. And it is here that the third and most serious difficulty is reached. In our Eurocentric view, three-quarters of our century too was dominated by the rise and fall of the Modern Movement. And this is an enigmatic situation, for Modernism was either the last ideology in architecture, or it may even now be gathering strength and influence for a resurgence in the decades, if not the centuries to come.

To review a century of architecture is to confront these issues head-on, and to go down before them. To the first charge of subjectivity, all must plead guilty. To the second charge of Eurocentrism, culpability again. Until the advent of jet travel and colour photography, architectural history lacked the means of global reach, let alone the will, and such a tradition of myopia is hard to shake off. Even today the vast majority of the buildings illustrated in architectural books and magazines are European or North American. In this sense the Anglo-Saxon world, with its own particular aspirations for and restraints upon architecture, has been made to do a job that another viewpoint might have transformed into something different. But again, it is the particularities of the culture of architecture that make up its history and provide the signposts that we recognize when we explore it.

How then do we plead on the third charge, the charge that European architectural history allows the rise and fall of the Modern Movement to ride roughshod over virtually our whole century? Here we offer a defence. Modern architecture was a magnificent mutiny against historicism, revivalism and the vernacular. It presented our century with a culture of buildings that identified them as instruments instead of monuments. This is the kernel of the idea that bestrides twentieth-century architecture like a colossus. In all its decades, from the Edwardian age to the Internet, its presence is central, whether as *avant garde*, rising tendency, revolutionary challenge, global orthodoxy, unmitigated evil or (perhaps) as fallen giant.

During all these years the struggle between the past and the future reflected the enormous pressure of four key historical events. In chronological order these were: the destruction of the old empires of Europe and creation of new republics in the aftermath of the Great War; the suppression of Modern architecture in Germany and the Soviet Union during the 1930s and the consequent dispersal of its most gifted practitioners; the overthrow of the forces of Fascism at the end of the Second World War and the consequent global triumph of Modernism and rejection of Neoclassicism; and finally the shock administered to the Keynesian economies of the Western world by the oil price increases of 1973–9 and the changing balance of power which they heralded. Changes which swiftly led to the wholesale dismantling of public sector spending programmes. Today, on the brink of the Millennium, what remains of Modernism is at the mercy of a fifth challenge, the most powerful of all. That challenge is one of perception. For events are changing the meaning of architecture into something that may no longer be identifiable as a set of beliefs or principles at all.

Only in the last years of this century has it become possible to identify a new cause with the power and universality to reinvigorate the Modern crusade. This contender, once again driven by the idea of function, is 'Green Architecture'. Its driving force is the principle that architectural form should be dictated by compliance with the global energy and

113

environmental imperatives that govern human survival. Despite, or because of, this awesome responsibility, the 'Green Architecture' movement has as yet no definitive architectural incarnation and seldom rises above the level of mass under glass with add-on components. It exists only as a series of disconnected experimental or near-experimental structures; solar and naturally ventilated buildings for the most part, all woefully under-researched for the immensity of the transformation they are expected to complete. The long-term prospects of this movement are as problematic today as the prospects for Modern architecture must have seemed 100 years ago.[1]

Setting aside the challenge of 'Green Architecture', this is the story of the last quarter of our century, a period during which the struggle between the two principal architectural ideologies has dissolved into an uneasy synthesis wherein 'quality' is held to be discernable in all styles, and the term 'style' itself has progressively shed its historic role as a rallying point for rival movements. In some ways this condition, which might be characterized as an 'architectural unbelief system', is reminiscent of the last decade of the imperial era before 1914, with 'Green Architecture' playing the part of nascent Modernism and posing the same potential threat to the academic and art-historical ideas of the professional establishment. But in other more important ways it represents unexplored territory, less likely to see reruns of the set-piece

After a generation the image of the famous 'Drop City' domes, built in New Mexico in the 1960s, still points towards a meeting point of disurbanization and 'Green Architecture' in the future.

Symbolic of the exodus from Modernism, a queue of East German Trabant cars waits to cross the frontier into Czechoslovakia in 1989. The body of the Trabant, made of cotton reinforced phenolic resin, survives in an improved form in a type of cladding used for buildings.

battles between function and decoration, or permanence and ephemeralism, than to convoy the entire meaning of the word 'architecture' to another destination altogether.

It is important when allowing Modernism its due precedence in recent history not to neglect the strength of the opposing views that were most forcefully presented during two great periods of attack: the first at the hands of the neo-classical totalitarian European regimes of the 1930s; and the second by the royalist Classical Revival movement of the 1980s. This is necessary because, while it may seem in the closing years of the twentieth century that the echoes of both these great conflicts have died down, and the literature of the present has become adulatory and superficial by comparison, the work of architectural historians and theorists, like the writings of philosophers, fluctuate in their perceived cruciality. Some writers believe even now that the ashes of the old-style wars remain hot enough to re-ignite a combat. Others see the exhaustion of polemical architectural theorizing as a reflection of the decline in the status and intensity of architectural ideas in general, from the high point of their conviction and urgency at the end of the Second World War to their present dismal consumerization.

The purpose of this chapter is to interpret the transition from style wars to 'inclusivism',[2] beginning with a summary of the relationship between architecture and the three main episodes in European history that comprise the century itself.

These are the Imperial Age, which ended in 1914; the Modern Age, which ran from 1919 to 1973; and the post-Modern Age, which began in the 1970s and still continues.

The Imperial Age in architectural history extends into the early twentieth century but is dominated by the issues of the nineteenth century and before. It remains the last era to have been held in undisputed thrall to the authority of the past, even though its vision of it was heavily romanticized and subject to extreme distortions. Despite this exploitation of its plasticity, the past was the principal reference for all nineteenth-century architectural theory. Even the tremendous achievements of Victorian engineering were clouded by an allegiance to the aesthetic prejudices of the time, and all the architectural theorists of the Imperial Age concerned themselves principally with aesthetic issues. Technique, in this respect, was relegated to a subsidiary, non-artistic literature of its own. Thus it became possible to revive Gothic architecture as a style, and pointlessly dissect it into such esoteric subdivisions as Early Christian, Romanesque, Early Italian Renaissance, Italian Gothic, Egyptian, Mesopotamian and Baroque, while ignoring (say) the architectural implications of long-span engineering structures. There was similarly little or no connection between the radical political ideas of the time and the conception of architectural forms to express them. The principal architectural theorists of the era were not revolutionaries, except in so far as this word can be applied to neo-feudal craft-socialism or a dogged defence of Gothic architecture. This was the stance of William Morris (1834–96), Augustus Welby Pugin (1812–52), John Ruskin (1819–1900) and others, none of whom seriously endeavoured to address the social or technical challenges of the day in terms that would be thought sensible today.

In England, only towards the very end of the nineteenth century did emphasis upon the expression of truth, honesty and craftsmanship in building begin to give place to a macroscopic level of thinking, and when it did the issues raised were connected with ambitious urban projects, like London's 'Imperial Processional Way' proposed at the turn of the century to reach from Buckingham Palace to the Guildhall via two new Thames bridges and a monster 'Imperial Parliament' on the South Bank. These and other grandiloquent projects are described in Thomas Metcalf's book *An Imperial Vision* and make a worthy comparison with the nascent Modern notions inspired by revolutionary events and utopian writings originating on the European mainland. The latter's echo in England was relatively muted, but nonetheless, among the leading figures responding to these new ideas, were writers who were to wield world influence. These included the pioneer of town planning, Ebenezer Howard (1850–1928), whose seminal volume *Tomorrow: A Peaceful Path to Real Reform*, launched the garden city movement, and his contemporary Patrick Geddes (1854–1932), whose *City Development* and *Cities in Evolution*[3] took a more politicized view, foreshadowing much twentieth-century social engineering. A parallel figure in architecture was William Lethaby (1857–1931), whose *Architecture, Mysticism and Myth* anticipated aspects of the later seminal text of modern architecture, Le Corbusier's *Vers une architecture* of 1923, although to a lesser extent than the work of Adolf Loos (1870–1933), whose collected polemical essays were published in Vienna in 1897 and 1898 and only later translated into English.

The balance of influence in favour of tradition did not change with the advent of the new century. Most mainstream architectural writing in the fourteen years before the outbreak of the Great War continued to lean heavily on the recycled historicism of the revivalists. In this river of mainstream aesthetic inspirations non-political aesthetic movements like Art Nouveau and the Vienna Secession joined the dominant Greek, Roman and Gothic Revival styles to be subsumed into an exotic Edwardian literature informed by the grandeur and triumphalism of colonial empires. As in the last decade of the nineteenth century, proto-Modern writings continued to appear, but the importance they have been accorded in recent years is anachronistic. So much so that today early twentieth-century polemicists like the Italians Antonio Sant'Elia (1888–1916) and Mario Chiattone (1891–1957), and the authors of the *Futurist Manifesto* of 1914, enjoy a posthumous importance that is entirely the creation of hindsight and art-historical research. In the mainstream world of European architecture in the years to 1914 their significance was negligible. If there was an emphasis on progress elsewhere than in Britain, it was focused not on the European Modernist *avant garde* but on the spectacular high-rise construction and large-scale industrial building that was taking place in the United States of America.

Because of the sheltered dissonance of its own literature, it is only in retrospect that we can see how the distinctive architecture of the last decades of the Imperial Age was in effect 'ghosted' by engineers and made possible by the performance of the new materials of nineteenth-century engineering, steel, concrete and plate glass. The first recognition that a deception of some kind had been perpetrated by the art historians of the Victorian age in this regard arose later. A characteristic example could be found in the view of the pre-1914 period taken by the critic John Betjeman when he wrote disparagingly in *Ghastly Good Taste* of 'a pre-war system that allowed "gentlemen" to show off their knowledge of period, while the all-important engineers had their good work hidden'.

The second ideological era of the twentieth century was dominated by the rise of the Modern Movement. This was an epoch ushered in by the Great War and strangely intensified during the turbulent twenty years' peace that followed. It was then brought to triumphant fruition in the aftermath of the Second World War, when Modern ideas in art, architecture and politics were finally fused together into an ideology combining elements of communistic and socialistic social order with functional industrial design, radical town planning and social architecture – all preoccupations that had been merely *avant garde* enthusiasms during the Edwardian era.

In a manner that is even more visible today than it was when Betjeman wrote, we can see that it was not merely a wilful concealment of engineering work that ended with the Great War, but the whole process of craft continuity once enshrined in ancient guild apprenticeships and pupillage. In the course of the war the exact relationships of rank, order and responsibility that had governed the operations of the Victorian construction industry were swept away. The magnitude of the change was so vast that it took a later generation of historians, notable among them the incisive Niels Prak in his *Architects: The Noted and the Ignored*, to unravel the way in which an entirely new era of construction began as a result of the war.

It has become difficult to grasp the scale of the disaster that the Great War of 1914–18 represented for the Imperial Age. In addition to a death toll of more than 35 million soldiers and civilians, the struggle swept away the accumulated territories, social and administrative systems, and social and cultural assumptions of three great empires: imperial Germany, imperial Austria-Hungary and imperial Russia. With them went a continuity in architectural thought that generations of conservative theorists and practitioners have striven in vain to re-create ever since.

This break in continuity can be likened to a mutiny, which begins amid the ashes of the first great European struggle and only really succeeds after the descent of European civilization into another even greater episode of destruction twenty years later. In architecture this mutiny begins with a repudiation of nineteenth-century art-historical thinking and ends with the emergence of a new form of architectural patronage through the state. The great state-funded programmes for social betterment belong to this period, as do the great ideological manifestos of Modernism, the best popularizing Modernist texts, and also the most savage denunciations from the historicist camp, thrown onto the defensive for the first time.

Compared to, say, the reintroduction of the Greek Revival style – whether in its Regency or Edwardian manifestation – the arrival of Modern architecture represented a vast upheaval. This was an evolutionary change rather than a minor aesthetic event. So grand indeed were its tremors, and so tragic its end that it bears comparison with such events as the rise and fall of the dinosaurs, rather than any possible exaggeration of the differences between columns, windows or mouldings that had previously served to identify architectural styles. To understand the difference between Modern architecture and any of the sub-variants of Greek or Gothic Revival, we have to accept that it was a phenomenon of a different order, one less related to the design of individual buildings than to the grand strategy of fulfilling the accommodation needs of mass societies, mobilized by war.

The interaction of the two wars (recovery from one and preparation for the next, followed by recovery from the second) created a vast trauma lasting some 40 to 50 years in Europe. This was the period that brought about the final triumph of

Modern architecture by the Darwinian route of radical changes in the 'genetic frequency' of important building types. This in turn was the cause of massive changes in the 'genetic frequency' of certain approaches to design. Just as the great Ice Ages changed the species population in both affected and unaffected areas through migration, so did the great upheaval of the wars change architecture.

In the course of the two wars many hundreds of thousands of buildings were destroyed, maintenance and new construction ceased, and material and manpower shortages persisted long after each of the conflicts was over. In Europe and Asia the direct effect of the second war upon the countries involved lasted for at least half a century; in some ways it still persists. As a direct consequence of aerial bombardment, land warfare and neglect, massive post-war building programmes were undertaken to produce housing, schools, hospitals and factories. During this period of accelerated construction, revolutionary new designs, building materials and techniques which minimized material and manpower input gained within a few years a prominence that they would not otherwise have attained in a century. The old craft-enthralled 'shape' of the profession of architecture was bent to new social and political ends: its practitioners (and their apologists) were made to make the desperate culturally acceptable. And they did so.

The situation at the end of the Second World War was truly a moment of crisis, and in response to it the tradition of all that had gone before was jettisoned in all save its practically useless art-historical outlines. Experience of traditional materials and methods could not compete with a desperate need for new ones. In an unprecedented rupture, the wisdom of the old building trades was thrown away and the profession of architecture began to re-educate itself from the scientific laboratory.

Looking back on the years immediately before the Second World War in his monograph *Architectural Criticism in the 1930s*, the architectural critic James Richards (1908–92) wrote:

It might almost be said of architectural criticism in England in the 1930s that there was none – none, at least, in the sense of regular appraisals of new buildings as they were put up. Why not? There were, I think, two main reasons. The first was that architecture had come to be regarded as a professional mystery, and so much emphasis was put on new planning and building techniques and new aesthetic allegiances that only those within the move-ment – only in fact architects – were thought to be qualified to act as critics, and most architects were inhibited by the professional man's reluctance to infringe etiquette by criticizing his fellow practitioners.

The other, perhaps more fundamental obstacle to the regular practice of architectural criticism was the impor-tance attached at this time to principle rather than example. The qualified writers were concerned with polemical arguments about Modernism. They were dedicated to a cause, and not only did they regard the kind of building that did not adhere to the cause they believed in to be unworthy of serious criticism – or only worthy of being dismissed as wrong-headed rather than discussed in rela-tion to its own terms of reference – but also they could not allow themselves to approach at all critically the buildings that did adhere to their cause for fear of weakening or betraying it.

It is worth quoting this passage at length because it exactly identifies the difference between criticism of performance and criticism of intention that has been central to the literature of architecture in the twentieth century. Richards is dismissive of ideological criticism because it takes sides and does not concern itself with performance, only with propaganda. The case seems unanswerable and yet it flies in the face of what we know intuitively to be true. The period between the wars was a period of ideological struggle, but it also saw the appearance of the best and most influential buildings of the twentieth century.

Modern architecture attained world domination in an environment of catastrophe, flaunting its new powers as the silver lining of the thunder clouds of war. From the beginning it was driven by a spirit of radical innovation that dwarfed what might be called the isolated 'genetic experiments' of the Imperial Age. By 1945 these experiments had so far proved themselves as to share the status of 'Modern medicine', even 'Modern science'. As a result, in the crucial post-war decade 'Modern architecture' was accepted in the utilitarian spirit of

The environment created by high-density living in the 1960s. Part of a large South London public housing project under construction.

rationing, popular mobilization, mass production and planning, and therein lay the seeds of its downfall.

Modern architecture brought order to the built environment. With their design methodology and new technology to match, modern architects made order possible where tradition had buckled at the knees. Properly trained, a modern architect could design anything, from a thousand houses to a concert hall, simply by arranging the activities that would go on inside and putting a 'go anywhere' flat roof over the top. The capacity to impose order in this way gave architects tremendous authority at a time when neglect, destruction and shortages had reduced much of the infrastructure of daily life to incoherence. It was nearly 30 years before changing circumstances were to remind them that all this new-found indispensibility depended on the government's capacity to keep the same sort of order in the national economy.

Meanwhile, many thousands of architects were being trained as rapidly as possible and sent out to practise their art. In Britain the number of registered architects rose rapidly, from 6,000 to 20,000 in the twenty years from 1945. The new planning profession called for the construction of 200 New Towns, the removal of industry to parts of the country with high unemployment and the construction of a 2,000-mile motorway network to link everywhere to everywhere else. All this work was begun by the 1950s, but much of it was delayed, ill-synchronized and poorly executed. For decades public sector administrations and nationalized industries cushioned incompetence, overmanning, poor management, lack of skills and obsolescence in everything from education to ship-building. It was upon this Byzantine structure of ambitious, wasteful and sluggish state-driven enterprise that the energy crisis, the stock market crash and the great inflation of the 1970s descended like a biblical plague.

When, on the 6th of October 1973, engineering units of the Egyptian army fought their way across the Suez Canal and surged into the Israeli-occupied Sinai desert, they inadvertently began the post-Modern Age. Through an elaborate sequence of events their actions, which led to the quintrupling of the price of Arab oil and the spectre of fuel starvation in the United States, created an economic crisis which dealt the high-energy economies of the Western world a savage blow.[4] Slowly at first but with gathering speed they began to curtail the high levels of government spending on social welfare that had become established since the Second World War. As part of this economy drive that affected all Western countries, the construction of new schools, hospitals, universities and public housing was cut back. The blow to the profession was savage. By the end of the decade Modern architecture was fighting for its life.

Northaird Point in the London Borough of Hackney, was ordered to be dynamited in 1985, but its upper half survived the collapse with even its window glass intact. This event contributed to the end of a spate of public sector demolitions likened by some to public executions.

Despite emerging from the Second World War as an unchallenged symbol of planning, social welfare and democracy, with a mandate to rebuild devastated cities everywhere, Modern architecture could not survive without state spending. By the late 1960s half the profession in Britain was employed in the public sector and half of the private sector survived on public sector commissions. In the aftermath of the oil embargo, when Western governments had already been forced by energy costs into hyperinflation and desperate cuts in public spending, social architecture swiftly succumbed. With a great unfairness all the more inexplicable with the passage of time, and which its erstwhile practitioners never seemed able to explain, Modern architecture then fell into deep disgrace. Architects were blamed for the shortcomings of all the new construction techniques like flat roofs, prefabricated elements and system building. Some of the worst episodes of a long period of opprobrium occurred in the early 1980s, taking the form of the addition of pitched roofs to hundreds of units of flat-roofed local authority housing, and the dynamiting of poorly maintained tower blocks on the grounds that they were 'socially undesirable'. These last events were curiously popular, being attended by masses of people in an atmosphere described by one observer as reminiscent of a public hanging.[5]

The shock to the profession of Modern architecture's disgrace was akin to an insider's view of the failure of a bank. First there was a stunned silence, then a panic-stricken rush to evade blame. Finally human nature asserted itself and the coolest heads began an attempt to make a new life out of whatever architecture was left. It was at this last stage that it became clear that there were three if not four futures still available, all of them cleansed of the ideological associations that had at first been the making, and were now the breaking, of the Modern Movement.

The first and least complicated of these involved a return to fundamentalism, swallowing whole the nineteenth-century revivalist conviction of the superiority of the past as a source of inspiration and a safeguard against unpopularity. Although somewhat discredited by association with the architectural taste of the recently defeated dictators, Classical Revival architecture proved to have more adherents than had been imagined, not least among the popular membership of the conservation movement, a collection of grass-roots voluntary organizations the strength of whose underlying philosophy was brilliantly encapsulated in a 1981 *Times* leader: 'The thing a building most needs to secure public affection is to have been standing a very long time. This is a quality hard to achieve in new construction.' Hard, perhaps, but not impossible. Within a decade of the oil embargo the conservation coalition of amateur historians, charitable foundations and government-funded quangos had expanded to occupy the vacant chairs of the planners, designers and visionaries of the utopian years. By the end of the 1980s a strongly conservationist heritage culture had already consolidated its position as the dominant ethos of local planning and development control in Britain. Its watchdog voluntary societies were organized into a seamless network of enthusiasts represented at government level by English Heritage, a publicly funded umbrella organization.

At the pointed end of this heritage culture, damaged far

At the height of the Prince of Wales-led Classical Revival of the mid-1980s, architect Robert Adam designed this 'Classical skyscraper' because, as he said, 'The Romans would not have hesitated to do it if they had had modern materials.'

APOLLO TOWER
ROBERT ADAM

less than their Modernist cousins by the loss of public sector spending on public housing, hospitals and suchlike, were a handful of determinedly Classical designers who had fought their way through schools of architecture in the face of jeering Modernists and now found that their modest private commissions for gazebos and small country houses had begun to excite envy among their contemporaries. From the early 1980s onward this group endeavoured to carry out a variety of modern commissions in the spirit (and as far as possible using the methods) of the eighteenth century. Probably the best known of these architects, Quinlan Terry (1937–), not only designed neo-Georgian country houses but went on to design large office buildings of externally Georgian appearance in London and Richmond, together with a number of prestige university buildings. Another Classical Revivalist, the leading theorist of the group, Robert Adam (1948–), even designed a Classical skyscraper on the grounds that 'the Romans would not have hesitated to do it if they had had modern materials'. But this project was never put to the test.

Adherence to the cause of conservation and historical correctness was not confined to true believers. There were economic inducements as well. By the mid-1970s no less than 20,000 architects had been trained since the war for the Modern mission of 'designing a new and organized surface of the earth',[6] a job that was no longer considered necessary or even desirable. Many of them used their enforced periods of leisure to reconstruct their perception of recent events, put away their utopian plans and seek modest conservation projects instead. There were compensations for surrendering to the past in this way. Many highly respected Modern architects did not hesitate. They rapidly became experts in historic construction techniques and received commissions from heritage clients.

By the peak of the 1980s economic boom the combined conservation and heritage organizations of Britain, reinforced by tourist earnings, were disbursing large sums of money in the shape of grants and loans for the restoration, repair and 'sympathetic' enlargement alterations to historic buildings. All architects were eligible for this kind of work and, although the pickings were slimmer than those of the great post-war public housing programmes, there were sizeable commissions to be won. For those prepared to pore over *Gwilt's Encyclopedia of Architecture* in search of authentic details, it was as though the Modern Movement had never happened.

If collaboration with heritage conservation and Classical Revival was the first course of action open to those cast away by the wreck of Modern architecture, this was only because it had survived in a meagre form from the end of the Imperial Age right through the period of Modern domination and emerged intact at the end of it. Its opposite was the fragment of Modern orthodoxy that survived the wreck of the public sector majority and went on to establish itself as an elite on a global scale. This was a meritocratic alternative, available only to a limited number of architects, for it required great design ability with little room for compromise. In return for enduring competition so cutthroat that it drove drawing office salaries down to levels not seen since the end of pupillage, this option offered the lucky ones challenging work on advanced technology buildings for private sector clients.

Called 'High-Tech', a term derived from a 1970s American style of interior decoration that made use of wall-painted supergraphics, tables made out of racing car wheels, industrial lighting, cable-tray shelving and suchlike non-domestic items, this approach to architecture relied on new materials,

Completed in 1976, the Bravo platform on the Shell/Esso Brent Field in the North Sea represents the tip of a submerged skyscraper. The platform is 251 metres above the sea bottom upon which it stands.

adventurous engineering and fastidious attention to details. Characterized by structurally expressive cold-moulded steel frames, mast-supported or cable-braced roofs, superplastic, teflon-coated fabric, glass, composite or profiled metal cladding, electrophoretic coatings, esoteric adhesives and polycarbonate glazing, this architecture started out looking like the heavy steel frame and glass style refined by Mies van der Rohe 50 years before, but rapidly evolved into a much lighter, more precise and elegant minimalism so seductive that, years after its debut, it was taken up by the administrators of grand historic buildings as the appropriate style for extensions and additions.

It is difficult to assign an exact date to the transition from 'old' Modern to new 'High-Tech' architecture, although the possible starting points are legion. At one level it can be said that the superstructure of any warship from the late nineteenth century onwards features a montage of accommodation reminiscent of the 'High-Tech' Inmos semiconductor factory, or the prominent service towers of the Lloyds Building in London, both designed by Richard Rogers (1933–). The later interiors of warships with enclosed bridges and large quantities of internal electronic equipment are even more akin to 'High-Tech' buildings, as are the offshore oil and gas platforms[7] built in British yards for the North Sea in some numbers from the late 1970s.

Depending on the looseness of the criteria employed, contenders for the first 'High-Tech' building can be as old as the 1858 Sheerness Boat Store, designed by the engineer Geoffrey Greene, or as recent as the Reliance Controls building of 1967 – the last work of the short-lived partnership of Richard Rogers and Norman Foster and the starting point recommended by Colin Davies in *High-Tech Architecture*.[8] If light metal construction is considered to be the crucial ingredient, then there are contenders from the 1930s, notably the steel and glass 'Crystal House' designed for the 1934 Chicago 'Century of Progress' exhibition by George Fred Keck (1895–1980). A very early shot at a larger 'High-Tech' public building, on the scale of the Centre Pompidou or Lloyds of London, was the competition-winning project for the Danish Trades Union Congress Hall by Gunnar Krohn (1900–77), which won the Gold Medal of the Royal Danish Society of Architects in 1941 but was never built. With its tapered perforated steel

One of last designs executed by Mies van der Rohe before his death in 1969, this London tower project, which included a new public square, was defeated by concerted conservationist opposition at a public inquiry in 1985.

Occupying part of the same site as the Mies van der Rohe scheme, this low-rise Postmodern replacement by James Stirling was completed in 1997.

beams, glass cladding and cable-supported *porte-cochère* it anticipated many later 'High-Tech' features.

While in the end all searches for a progenitor will probably be inconclusive, the rise in status of 'High-Tech' architecture during the last quarter of the twentieth century is indisputable. Today it is indissolubly associated with the careers of the English architects Sir Norman Foster (1935–), Lord Rogers, Nicholas Grimshaw (1941–), Michael Hopkins (1941–), Eva Jiricna (1938–), Ian Ritchie (1947–) and others – whose very survival during the 'purification' of the 1970s and 1980s had tenuously depended on foreign clients, on working overseas and on overseas commissions. These architects are now renowned the world over as exponents of 'The English Style', fêted and promoted by the British government at home and overseas as masters of the new, ideology-free face of Modern architecture.

As another indication of how the status of 'High-Tech' has changed it is worth recalling that as recently as 1985, when the heritage classicists allied to Prince Charles were powerfully in the ascendant, Richard Rogers took part in a debate at the Oxford Union. It was not a portentous affair, taking place in front of an audience in the Union library rather than the debating chamber, but the event and its outcome are worth recounting. The motion was 'This house believes that the goal of Modern art is suicide and death'. It was proposed by the doyen of Classical Revivalists, Quinlan Terry, and opposed by Rogers.

Tall and formal in bearing, and dressed in a worn country suit of good quality, Terry spoke fluently without notes in the military manner, telling his audience what he was going to say, saying it, and then telling them what he had said. In a nutshell, he believed that Modern art and architecture were expressions of the alienation of twentieth-century machine society, and that all Modern artists were condemned to eventual madness and suicide.

Rogers sat through this bleak analysis riffling through his cue cards. Unlike Terry he was not dressed to meet his maker. Instead he wore moccasins, baggy chino trousers, an open-neck shirt and an Italian bomber jacket. When it was his turn to speak, he smiled nervously at the audience, rose to his feet, and dropped his cue cards on the floor. He recovered from this inauspicious beginning, but barely. Rogers has never been a confident public speaker and he is often unclear. But that night at the Oxford Union the audience understood him well enough. In a rambling, disconnected fashion he claimed to be a Modern artist; claimed that Picasso was as great a man as Michelangelo, and that Sigmund Freud was more than equal to Lord Burlington. As for Terry's indirect invitation to commit suicide, he had no intention of complying with it.

Terry sat through this performance ramrod straight, as he did through the inconsequential contributions from the floor that followed. When the vote was taken by a show of hands, to the amazement of connoisseurs of debating technique, Rogers won by a knockout. In the bar afterwards a journalist present asked several students from the audience why they had voted for him. One answer kept cropping up: 'He was wonderful. You could see how nervous he was. He was so nervous.'[9]

If Classical Revival and 'High-Tech' were rescue boats that reached the scene of the sinking of the SS *Modern Architecture* and saved many from professional eclipse, they may have been unaware that a much larger craft was on its way. One so big as to be able to pick up everyone left and more besides. This vessel was Postmodernism, a roomy ocean liner of a ship able to accommodate post-ideological tendencies in all the arts and professions.

Postmodernism is by far the largest and most multi-faceted phenomenon to emerge from the crisis of Modernism in the 1970s. In its broadest sense it comprises all subsequent tendencies in culture and the arts, literature and science as well. Unlike heritage conservationism, which is a mutated survival from an earlier age, or 'High-Tech', which is Modernism's elite obsession, Postmodernism is a great liberator. Given a clear run by art historians, who felt more than able to control any historicist excesses, it was able to spring Hydra-headed from a thousand points of origin in the aftermath of the mid-1970s world crisis. Furthermore, unlike the uncertain origins of 'High-Tech', its starting date in architecture was precise. Indifferent to the claims of Egyptian army engineers, Postmodernism's most indefatigable chronicler, the historian and theorist Dr Charles Jencks (1941–), insists in *The Language of Postmodern Architecture* that the birth date of post-Modern architecture is the date that Modern architecture died, an event that he equates with the blowing up of the Pruitt-Igoe public housing project in St Louis, Missouri, 'on July 15th 1972 at 3.32 p.m.'.

7 From Postmodernism to Terrorism

'Because London has a capacity to renew itself endlessly, most of the buildings of its twenty-first-century infrastructure are already in place. What architects have to do now is to change the meaning of these buildings to correspond to new realities.'

THEO CROSBY, 1987

A generation ago the late Charles Moore, considered along with Robert Venturi (1925–), Robert Stern (1939–) and the historian Vincent Scully to be a founding father of post-Modern architecture in America, published an essay about the future. 'If architects are to continue to do useful work on this planet,' he concluded, 'then their proper concern must be the creation of place. To make a place is to make a domain that helps people know where they are and, by extension, who they are.'

Moore's plea – that architecture should concentrate on history and context, rather than pick up clues from such global look-alikes as airports, factories, skyscrapers and auto routes – struck precisely the right note for the burgeoning anti-Modernism of the time. The tone that he adopted, modest yet apocalyptic, was widely imitated by other architects, particularly in America. It was the beginning of an era in which an architectural version of the confessional performance of the Nixon aides embroiled in the Watergate scandal[1] was to ignite the enthusiasm of students of architecture everywhere for the new creed of Postmodernism. The essence of the performance was an admission that Modernism had been a big mistake, but that from now on things were going to be different.

Architects with a past in Modern architecture toured American university departments and schools of architecture with this message in the 1970s, putting on the kind of interminable 'show and tell' that architects always do, but spicing it up by ripping into their early work with gusto, denouncing it as dehumanized, arrogant, bleak, anonymous, out of scale, forbidding, impoverished, a monstrous outburst of evil, and so on. This went down well but it was all for the sake of effect.

The slide show always ended with a talisman of the new recruit to Postmodernism's change of heart. An office tower bedecked with fake stone rosettes might do it, or the entrance to a shopping mall with attenuated columns and a pediment. Best of all would be evidence of real contrition, a watercolour sketch of a village in Tuscany. Whatever the last image was, all charges relating to 'dehumanization', etc., would immediately be dropped. Moore (1925–93), Stern, Michael Graves (1934–), Philip Johnson (1906–) and James Stirling (1926–92), among others, gave lectures like this. In every case the lecturer was shriven by the experience. Purged of the Modern infection. Free of guilt at last!

Yet within twenty years all these pioneers and reformed characters and their enthusiastic followers, with their plans to 'make places' by means of the humanity and historical openness of post-Modern architecture, had given birth to monsters.

Postmodernism sweeps all before it. A new apartment tower on the sea front at Funchal, Madeira, 1982.

Consider an apparently innocent nineteenth-century building in London. Today it is the European headquarters of Nomura International, the world's largest dealer in securities. It occupies an entire four-façade city block and was recently the subject of a £100 million refurbishment, the largest façade-retention project ever executed in Europe. The architects for this project were a firm called the Fitzroy Robinson Partnership, but in reality there is no living designer who can claim mastery over the whole building. One hundred years ago the same outer walls of the Nomura building housed a *five*-storey Royal Mail sorting office whose courtyards echoed to the clattering of horse-drawn Mail coaches. Today they enclose 46,000 square metres of air-conditioned electronic office floor-space on *ten* floors, four of them below ground. Completed in 1991, Nomura is a veritable 'stealth bomber' of a building. It looks like a Victorian post office, but its period exterior reveals no hint of its electronic heart.

The lack of an organic connection between inside and outside at Nomura is typical of post-Modern architecture and has close parallels in other fields of human endeavour. Just as geriatric medicine and surgery can prolong human life by miracle drugs, organ transplants and prosthetic devices – at inordinate cost and to grotesque effect – so can post-Modern architecture preserve old buildings while at the same time utterly destroying their identity. As a result we have come to terms with the appearance of 'spare-part buildings', just as we have come to terms with the existence of 'spare-part people'. They merge out of different elements and different periods into a homogenized, de-historicized urban scene.

As a second example consider a building called 'The Queen's House'. This is a former royal palace attributed to the architect Inigo Jones (1573–1652) and located in the London Borough of Greenwich. Now a tourist attraction, it was built four centuries ago and has been several times refurbished, most recently by experts in historic architecture at a cost of £40 million. As a result it now holds several dubious world records. It is the only seventeenth-century building with fibre-optic lighting; the only royal palace with laser-scanned photographic prints stuck on in place of what were painted ceilings; and the only seventeenth-century building equipped with seventeenth-century reproduction furniture made in 1990.

The unpredictable vagaries of bomb damage. Only the front façade of this street in Exeter survived Luftwaffe bombing in 1942.

Today we think nothing of it when we look at an out-of-town media worker's terminal and see a farm worker's cottage. We look at a merchant bank and see a nineteenth-century church whose interior has been cunningly converted. We look at an apartment building and see what was once an eighteenth-century waterfront warehouse. In London we can even look at a Modern electronic office complex, complete with underground parking for 300 cars, and see a row of grand Georgian riverside houses.[2]

The adherence to historical architectural styles here is not the point. It is less important than the overlooked effects of the loss of organic integrity and the disappearance of meaning that flows necessarily from such projects. By this means, as though by a wilful collaboration with the force of electronically annihilated distance, all real places and all recognizable categories of building are disappearing: all authentic differences between historical architectural periods are being lost, and their 'strata' are being compressed as though by a tremendous seismic action. The urban environment reminds us of what the veteran American comedian George Burns once said of acting: 'The most important thing is honesty. Once you can fake that, you've got it made.'

The 'stealth building' is a fascinating artefact. Not so much a terminal as the final product of the pre-terminal age: the last combination of 'Terminal 1' and 'Terminal 2' in one schizophrenic structure, before the two value systems separate,

'Stealth' in architecture I. The façade of Nomura Properties plc's building at St Martin's le Grand in the City of London, which is leased by Nomura International, the world's largest dealer in securities. This former GPO head-quarters was gutted and reconstructed inside its four original Victorian façades, and extra floors were added. The architects were Fitzroy Robinson and Partners.

'Stealth' in architecture II. As this view of a dealing-room floor inside the Nomura building shows, the inside of St Martin's le Grand is entirely different from its outside. So much so that its exterior amounts to a kind of architectural 'Stealth' treatment, concealing the reality that lies behind.

once and for all. In this sense it is rich in an obsolete complexity, its antecedents stretching back into history. In one way the roots of its external appearance can be found in the architecture of pre-industrial, pre-electronic buildings, where hand-crafted details and bombastic ornament were whittled into a kind of usefulness again and again, over hundreds of years, with each stylistic makeover. In another way its vast open interior spaces can be traced back through the Miesian office towers of the Modern era to the barns and grain stores, industrial buildings, warehouses and 'Big Sheds' that make up today's inventory of styleless, historyless, cultureless, state-of-the-art 'Terminal 2' building envelopes.

Interestingly, there is a 'Terminal 2' explanation for the development of 'stealth architecture' that offers a technical analogue to all Charles Moore's nostalgia for place and identity and an end to the 'windswept plazas' of the Modern age. It rests upon the coterminous emergence of the first post-Modern buildings and the first successful 'stealth' aircraft, which were to become the United States Air Force F-117 fighter and the B-2 bomber, both of which, it is claimed, are impossible to detect by radar. The story of attempts to build undetectable aeroplanes can be traced back as far as the Great War, when experiments were carried out to try to develop a 'see-through' fabric covering for wooden aircraft that would make them transparent and thus invisible from the ground.[3] Because no transparent fabric was available that did not also shine in sunlight, this approach was abandoned in favour of various complex colour schemes designed to break up the outline of an aircraft or make it match the colour of the sky. In the event, the development of air power soon made it more important to camouflage aircraft while they were on the ground than when they were in the air, so this approach too was discontinued. Then with the introduction of radar in the 1940s another and much more certain risk of detection superseded eyesight altogether. Radar worked day and night over long ranges by bouncing electromagnetic waves off flying objects like reflections from a mirror. While it was early discovered that the signal bounced back to the radar transmitter differed considerably between different types of aircraft, notably in proportion to their size, at the time this 'radar signature' seemed to have little importance, for all propeller-driven aircraft gave off strong radar reflections from their whirling propeller blades. The only effective measure taken to reduce the power of radar was the practice of dropping quantities of reflective metallized paper to create an undifferentiated cloud of signals.[4]

It was only with the coming of jet engines and nuclear

ordnance at the end of the Second World War that the problem of evading radar detection received much more determined attention. The cross-sectional area of military aircraft was reduced as far as possible and 'soft' radar-absorbent coatings were developed to reduce the strength of the reflected signal. At the same time experiments were made with changes in the reflective angles of different parts of the aircraft's airframe so as to disperse incoming radar signals rather than reflect them back. While all these measures had some effect, none of them succeeded in solving the problem entirely. Military aircraft had always been designed within a performance envelope dominated by factors such as speed, range, carrying capacity, rate of climb and so on, and only then turned over to experts to be radar-proofed as far as possible. It was not until the late 1970s, by which time materials and systems technology and design calculations had been tremendously advanced by mean of computers, that the momentous decision was made to try to design a crew- and ordnance-carrying object that could not be detected by radar, *and then make it fly*, rather than the reverse.

Because of this conceptual breakthrough we can describe the American B-1 bomber as 'modern' because it was designed the old way – as a functional flying machine first and foremost, with secondary modifications to reduce its radar signature. But, as anyone who has seen its eerie shape moving through the air will confirm, its successor, the American B-2 'stealth bomber', is a truly 'post-Modern' aeroplane because

'Stealth' in the military I. The Rockwell International B-1B bomber, which entered service with the US Air Force in 1986, is essentially a Modern design for a high-performance military aircraft which has been given 'stealth' capability by means of limited redesign and the application of special non-reflective techniques.

'Stealth' in the military II. Unlike the B-1B, the F-117A, which entered service in 1983, is essentially a Post-modern design, conceived from the outset as a 'stealth' aircraft at the expense of many flying qualities. 'Stealth' buildings disguise their modernity in the same way as the F-117A, in their case sacrificing authenticity in the interests of a 'historical' appearance that is deemed more important.

it has been first and foremost designed to be undetectable by radar, and only secondarily made to fly.

Something similar to this evolutionary leap has also taken place in architecture, and it began to happen at almost the same time, in the late 1970s, when the same computerized overdevelopment of materials, methods and design skills had taken place in architecture. This made the International Style, trabeated-frame, curtain-walled Modern building – like the modern aircraft – an object that no longer presented a challenge to its designers. In the field of architecture the equivalent to the threat of radar detection was an increasing sentimental attachment by the public and the media to the historic context of these modern buildings and dissatisfaction with their incompatibility with it. To pursue the aviation analogy to the limit, the 'air' in which simple modern build-ings flew had also become hostile. In order to survive in this hostile critical environment, it was increasingly necessary for architects to devise 'criticism-absorbing forms' that had no place in the standard Modern canon. The truly post-Modern building is disguised on the outside in such a way as to mask its interior. It has no 'Modern signature', even though its interior – like the interior of the stealth bomber – contains a load of modern ordnance, in the case of the 'stealth building' a full complement of raised floors and false ceilings, work-stations, monitors and everything else that is necessary to make it a viable commercial proposition.

The combination of old and new and the separation of

interior and exterior were the crowning achievements of Postmodernism, but they must have come as a disappointment to Moore himself, who died in 1993. For by then they had led to another kind of 'International Style', the unmistakable silhouette of the giant mixed-use commercial development that can be found in every city from Berlin to Bangkok. These schemes, with their architecture of new versus old, interior versus exterior and plan versus elevation, are united only in their dedication to quantities of serviced floorspace just as universal and general and 'soulless' as anything ever associated with the excesses of Modernism. It is these buildings that have enabled the followers of Charles Moore to say that they really have 'helped people to know where they are and, by extension, who they are', for they have ensured that, appearances to the contrary, the prospects for Postmodernism remain as constrained as those of any other style.

From its inception in the early 1970s the ideology-free and internationalist post-Modern approach made it a veritable engine of patronage, moving architects, known and unknown, through to prestigious commissions, most notably perhaps Sir James Stirling, Frank Gehry (1929–), Michael Graves and Terry Farrell (1941–). Stirling, originally a Modernist with a track record in public sector housing and university commissions, and with a considerable following in Germany and America, represented an interesting case. In all the thousands of words written about him after his death, the most controversial aspect of his career, his repudiation of Modernism, was almost totally ignored, even though he himself was deeply scarred by it, conscious that it raised a number of questions about allegiance, ideology and leadership.

Like Winston Churchill, whose career his own resembled in certain ways, Stirling went in and out of fashion and changed his architectural politics more than once. Most importantly, he was among the very first architects of reputation to abandon Modernism in favour of a kind of post-Modern Neoclassicism, and so hasten the arrival of the pluralist approach to architecture that is dominant today. During the 1970s he employed two important Classical Revivalists in his office, Leon Krier (1946–) and Quinlan Terry, who appear to have influenced him more than he influenced them, for a decade later his curious No.1 Poultry Mansion

House Square project for Lord Palumbo, although not a 'stealth' design, clearly owed as much to Classical rudiments as it did to Modern pragmatism. Despite this, it was dismissed by the Prince of Wales as looking like 'a broken 1930s wireless set', from which sobriquet it has yet to recover.

In later years Stirling inveighed continually against the way in which critics and journalists pigeonholed all architects as Modernists, 'High-Tech', post-Modernists or Classicists. On one occasion at a discussion held at the Royal Academy he burst out, 'I hate and detest the labelling of cheap journalism. Labelling is a cheap and sloppy way of writing about architecture. Novelists are not dismissed as Modern, post-Modern, Classical Revival and so on. Why should architects be? A novelist is not a Modernist, a Post-Modernist or a Classicist,' he shouted. 'A novelist is a writer, a good or bad writer. That is all.'[5]

That he took this view with such vehemence seemed to indicate that he saw himself as a victim of classification. And if that were so, what could this perception reflect but the existence of still-open wounds sustained during his own controversial passage from Modernism to Postmodernism?

Sir James Stirling spent much time thinking about what critics thought of him, and the concern was reciprocated. For admirers of his Modern period, despite a dislike of his later work, he fulfilled too many of the critical requirements for greatness to be dismissed. At the same time he had failed a crucial test by not making a stand against an advancing tide of homogenization and compromise. He knew that this last was a view of him held by a certain generation. How he interpreted it can only be guessed: perhaps from his fulminations against classification; and perhaps also from the well-known inclusion in his book *James Stirling: Buildings and Projects* (1984) of a photograph of Le Corbusier autographed 'To Jim 29/8/65' – two days after the master's death.

James Stirling in person, as well as his work, inspired strong feelings. As strong, one is almost tempted to say, as Benedict Arnold. Modernism, like independence, was inextricably entwined with war. So much so that, for a certain generation, no able-bodied architect of the Modern era of military age who did not see service in either world war could ever be wholly admired. Those who did, and who survived, clearly knew and felt deeper things than other men. That this reasoning should have applied in architecture may seem inexplicable, but that it did was part of the now inexplicable charisma of the generation of 1914. Not merely Walter Gropius (1883–1969) and Richard Neutra (1892–1970), but such minor English figures as the once admired, now reviled Sir Basil Spence (1907–76), the architect of Coventry Cathedral, and the all-but-forgotten Lionel Brett (1913–). Measured against this ideal, former paratrooper James Stirling, who landed behind enemy lines on D-Day in 1944, was a hero. A man chosen by history to lead a generation. And yet he did not lead it.

The non-specific historicism of post-Modern design may have gone down well enough where even the most erudite critic saw no objection to Corinthian capitals and cyclopean masonry side by side – or 'more Venetian windows than there are in the whole of Vicenza' in a single building, as Philip Johnson proudly boasted of his enormous International Place complex in Boston – but in the end its greatest enemy is not to be found anywhere in the endless planar present in which it strives to dwell. Instead the threats to its survival come from the past and from the future.

Of the former, one need only note that there is a parallel between the preference shown by TV audiences for straight adaptations from literature in classic costume drama, and a similar popular preference for 'real' Classical Revival build-ings like Quinlan Terry's Richmond Riverside, as opposed to bizarre post-Modern compromises with Classicism like James Stirling's No.1 Poultry.[6] Of dangers from the future there are two. The second, which is far less trivial than the first, we shall return to. Of the first one might mention the growing influence of arts administrators over 'cultural' archi-tectural commissions, which is leading to the selection of an increasing number of thoroughly irrational designs. Certainly the greatest *succès d'estime* of Postmodernism in recent years have been achieved by the frankly irrational rather than the historical wing of the movement. Projects by Zaha Hadid (1950–) and Daniel Libeskind (1946–) in the form of angular compositions of planes shooting from a point have exploited a wholly artistic freedom of expression, best exemplified by the former's Vitra fire station at Weill (1995) and the latter's Holocaust Museum in Berlin (1998). Together with Hadid's Cardiff Bay Opera House project, and Libeskind's proposed extension to the Victoria and Albert Museum in London, all

'Stealth' in architecture III. This post-Modern office building in Basle, Switzerland, designed by Frank Gehry and completed in 1994, shows how far sacrifices in authenticity can go in pursuit of a branded identity.

of these projects betray a total dependency upon advanced structural engineering, computerized structural analysis and three-dimensional computer modelling. Without it such chaotic designs would be impossible to build.[7]

The continued coexistence of Classical Revival architecture, post-Modern architecture and 'High-Tech' since the mid-1970s confirms the last quarter of the twentieth century as a period of pluralism – not so much of consent, as in the years before 1914, nor of conflict, as in the inter-war years of 1919–39, but of nihilistic theorylessness. As its name suggests, the post-Modern Age is an age whose only ideology is the absence of historical chronology, an age in which all previous tendencies are allowed to coexist under the catch-all designation of 'contemporary architecture' through a mutual lack of conviction. The huge formal range and lack of discipline of post-Modern architecture, from near-authentic Classical replication to neo-sculptural *Star Trek* fantasy, has its roots in the openness of post-Modern designers to the deconstructing 'stealth' phenomenon.

It is in this sense that every configuration of post-Modern architecture has carried out Moore's instruction to the letter. It is perhaps a little disappointing to see a Chinese temple on top of what is obviously an American skyscraper, but it cannot be disputed that it tells you where you are and who you are. The only thing it will not tell you is that the survival of Postmodernism, claimed to represent the 'peace process' of the style wars, is nothing of the kind. No sooner did the struggle between internationalism and uniqueness appear to settle down to an uneasy compromise, than it became clear that the comparison between art history and a corrupt dictatorship is valid in more ways than one. Having played a masterly game of cat and mouse with the Modern mutineers, ending up by devouring them whole, art history unaccountably experiences more difficulty in digesting the complaisant, nay sacrificial, dish of Postmodernism.

The difference between Modernism and Postmodernism is, as they say, all in the presentation. But this is not so much a figure of speech as a literal fact. A massive change took place between the heyday of the Moderns in the 1950s and the rise of the post-Moderns in the 1970s. Chiefly this involved a reversal of the role of writing and photography in the communication of architectural ideas. While critics and commentators still strive to treat their subject with a great deal of seriousness, in the post-Modern era of saturated colour photography what they write has dwindled to a size and unreadability that mocks their efforts. 'Readers', leafing through glossy architectural magazines, no longer see text but a kind of grey Berber carpet between dazzling photographs and computer-generated images. In the same way detailed plans and sections of buildings, once considered an essential companion to published accounts in order to understand their purpose, are either used like wallpaper overprinted with text or withheld altogether in the interests of security.

The response to all this in the post-Modern world can only be described as illiterate fascination. Architectural writing may be cast into the outer darkness by four-colour photographic reproduction, digitized images, pastel-coloured computer-generated pie-charts and pages of tables with dots. Practising architects may feel more and more constrained by a cage of administrative restrictions – health and safety issues, building regulations, fire precautions and planning restrictions, crippling indemnity insurance. In the public mind none of this exists. The average newspaper reader believes that architects enjoy such occult powers that they require almost penal restraint.[8] Never mind that the average architectural picture book is now thinner than the average fashion magazine, nor that architecture and fashion are increasingly drifting towards a common ground of fantasy and illusion. The powers attributed to the architect in the public mind remain limitless.

In the last quarter of the twentieth century, the age of Postmodernism, architecture and fashion have come to take a synoptic view of the world. Neither depends on fresh thought or new discoveries: for the most part both survive by plagiarism and repetition. So much so that they rapidly lose their bearings when deprived of a steady diet of precedent and example. Because of this similarity, writing about fashion illuminates the weakness of theorizing about post-Modern architecture, and vice versa. Typically, in neither field does ceaseless repetition prevent critics from finding projects 'shocking', or detecting in them a 'New Look' (which is invariably either an old look subject to its latest re-release, or a look new only to the critic who finds it so). In the same way, both are alike in their capacity to arouse fickle, occasionally passionate but always ill-informed public debate. The means employed to stimulate this debate never change: it is invariably characterized by exaggeration, oversimplification and contradiction.

Examples come readily to mind. When a fashion historian generalizes wildly in *Fashion and Morality* that 'The best dressers of every age have always been the worst men and women', the statement, in its glib and sweeping unprovability, is a perfect example of the genre. It has its perfect counterpart in Jean Nouvel's declamation, 'I would not only die for architecture, I would kill for it.'[9] Or Richard Buckminster Fuller's solemn statement, 'The answer to the housing problem lies on the way to the Moon.'[10] Or Sir Norman Foster's alerting us (in a 1995 advertisement for Rolex watches) to the fact that he can glance at his 'and know exactly what the time is, just by the position of the hands'. The self-cancelling announcement in *Vogue*, 'Miniskirts are back, but don't panic. There's so much flexibility this season that you can vamp it up in asymmetrics and stilettos one day and wear a trouser suit the next',[11] is scarcely more oxymoronic than the opaque axioms of the great Modern pioneers: Mies van der Rohe's 'Less is more', or Le Corbusier's 'In architecture there is no such thing as detail, everything is important.'[12]

Recklessness, unconscious triviality and unmerited omniscience are endemic among fashion writers, designers, post-Modern architects and the people who write about them alike. At the heart of all of them is an unmistakable streak of amateurism, a significant trait of character that gives much away, for architecture, like fashion, is a business with a large amateur following endowed with an exaggerated idea of its importance in the world.

There is one final interesting reflection on the indigestibility of architectural theorizing to be drawn from the comparison of fashion and architecture. Notwithstanding their far greater cost and unconscionable gestation time compared to any creation of the fashion industry, the works of post-Modern architecture that are most exhaustively written about, like the collections of clothes that are most extravagantly admired, tend to be functionally dubious and well out of the economic mainstream. Michael Graves's 1981 Public Services building in Portland, Oregon, survived a bare twelve years before it was vacated and demolished, Nigel Coates' 1986 Caffe Bongo in Tokyo only two before being made over by another architect.

These acclaimed masterpieces of their genre exactly parallel the exclusive collections of *haute couture*. They were scandalous, much illustrated and much praised, but seldom seen. Their very inaccessibility enhanced their chance of fame. Just as fashion designers will use obscure Mongolian yarns, laboratory synthetic fabrics or unusual dyeing procedures, so will architectural historians and critics, eager to build up their own stable of talent, stake their reputations on rank outsiders or assiduous networkers in the right places. In this sense there is no excess of fashion that architecture cannot match. Just as the items of historical dress pillaged by fashion designers lack all authenticity of context, so are the most admired works of architecture, the building blocks of critical theory, often not even seen by those who write about them or use them as stepping stones in argument. The most often cited example is the original German pavilion designed by Mies van der Rohe for the Barcelona International Exposition of 1929, but there are others. The Japanese post-Modernist Arata Isozaki (1931–), for example, was awarded the Gold Medal of the Royal Institute of British Architects in 1986 by a panel of assessors, none of whom had ever seen a building he designed. Such is the power of the image cascade in the world of architecture and fashion, and such is the small importance accorded to the real thing.

Today, newly completed buildings whose designers aspire to cultural recognition are carefully marketed. They are pre-

146

Part of the Berlin Wall photographed on the Western side in 1987. The 'death strip' was visible from the small observation deck.

sented first to specially selected groups of people, groups on the whole evenly made up of potential patrons, potential critics and photographers. The critical notices that result from these select *vernissages* are no more enlightening than the breathless writing that results from exclusive fashion shows. Shrill, partisan and for the most part unreadable after the passage of a week or two, both rapidly fade into insignificance. Such un-art-historically acceptable writing makes up the bulk of the explication of post-Modern architecture. The authentic literature of architecture, written by or about architects by individuals with sufficient technical understanding, authority and judgement to understand the real issues, constitutes an infinitesimal part of the whole. It may be, by definition, the purest and most effective part, but it is crowded out by an indiscriminate flood of unmerited praise, all of which has served to obscure the changes that are taking place behind the scenes to subvert the purpose of architecture altogether.

It is time to return to the issue of the second threat posed by the future to Postmodernism, and indeed to architecture as a whole. No sooner did the struggle between internationalism and uniqueness appear to settle down to an uneasy compromise, with Postmodernism playing the part of a 'peace process', holding all sides together under the rubric of 'contemporary architecture', than another villain lumbered over

Damage caused by the April 1992 St Mary Axe bomb in the City of London. The GMW-designed Commercial Union building is on the left. The destruction inflicted by this bomb on the nearby Baltic Exchange created the site for the proposed London Millennium Tower.

the horizon. A villain more deadly by far to architecture than the mummified corpse of the Classical Revival, the supposed killjoy arrogance of Modernism and 'High-Tech', or the alphabet soup of Postmodernism itself. That this new villain is an 'ism' too is pure coincidence, but it is not a style. More accurately it is a death sentence upon styles. Its name is 'Terrorism', and it threatens to put paid to the game of 'making places' once and for all.

The architecture of terror comes from the universally acknowledged need to protect the highly serviced and vulnerable built environment of the modern world from attacks that fall short of declared war. Faced with the various terrorist threats which have to a large extent displaced the risk of military aggression in most of the developed world, governments, public utilities, banks, businesses and commercial property owners seek to safeguard their buildings by seeking the advice of military experts. Because the terrorist threat, far from evaporating, is gradually evolving into something like a continuous, low-intensity war, waged anywhere between the upper limits of vandalism and the lower limits of outright armed conflict, the influence of these security experts progressively increases. At first it comprised nothing more than the retrofitting of such crime prevention measures as steel shutters and closed-circuit video cameras, but its influence soon became more pervasive. It began to move back up the chain of command to the level of directives: on the selection of building materials and components; on the drafting of new regulations, the introduction of design guidelines and the control of planning decisions about every aspect of development. Now it determines the alignment and positioning of roads and the siting of buildings to make attack difficult, and imposes secret measures designed to make post-attack escape impossible. In Northern Ireland overall security planning of this kind began a quarter of a century ago and continues to this day.[13]

Once such a regime is inserted into the building control process, it is difficult to withdraw it. After design suggestions and guidelines come design directives. When the level of terrorist attack rises sharply, or the damage it causes leads to massive insurance claims, calls for further measures to 'design out terrorism' become impossible to resist. This is precisely what happened after the 1993 and 1994 one-tonne IRA truck bombs in the City of London, which inflicted £1.5 billion of damage, and the 1996 bomb at Canary Wharf which led to insurance claims of over £300 million. It also happened in the United States after the 1993 World Trade Center, 1995

Damage caused by a car bomb that exploded in Gloucester Street, Belfast, in November 1993. The high vulnerability of glass cladding is obvious.

Oklahoma, and 1996 Atlanta bombs. It happens after ETA attacks in Spain, after Tamil attacks in Sri Lanka, Palestinian attacks in Israel and the Lebanon, and cult attacks on urban transportation systems in Japan.

In London the response to the heavy bombing of the financial district in the early 1990s was the overnight introduction of road blocks manned by armed police at all the main entry points to the City. Within a year these were made permanent and incorporated into pedestrianization schemes as part of the City's urban design. Drastic as this 'Berlin Wall' around the City was, it was only one of a number of restrictions imposed on the use of urban space in London in the interests of security by the insertion of 'water-tight doors' to protect certain quarters of the city from vehicular or unmonitored pedestrian access. Downing Street, a public right of way for centuries, in addition to being the home of the Prime Minister, was in 1986 closed off with permanent security gates and monitored by surveillance cameras. Within ten years the experience of living behind gates and beneath official scrutiny had become a daily reality for over a million city dwellers. The meaning of this transformation was cleverly defined by the artist Anne Eggebert, whose March 1994 exhibition at London's Royal College of Art consisted of video cameras fixed to the top of the college building and relay monitors suspended inside it. 'The cameras', she suggested, 'might be equated with the masterful gaze of colonists, whose supremacy reflects the continual scrutiny by a dominating nation of its colonial subjects.'[14]

In London the creation of urban 'exclusion zones' that began with the sealing off of Downing Street, and went on to meter road access to the City, is set to continue. Next in line to be built is a huge pedestrianized zone incorporating Trafalgar Square, the government offices in Whitehall and Horse Guards Parade, the Houses of Parliament and Parliament Square. This project, if it is ever executed, will mean massive traffic diversions, the loss of hundreds of parking spaces, the prevention of uncontrolled vehicle access anywhere within 200 metres of government offices, and the closure of Horse Guards Road in St James's Park to all save pedestrians and cyclists. Entrusted to Sir Norman Foster, and determinedly described as a scheme to improve the urban environment under the blithe name of 'World Squares for All', it will also

Responding to the continued terrorist threat in Northern Ireland, this building, designed by the BBC architects' department and opened in 1984, shows the effect of strict security measures on external design.

Another example of 'security' architecture in Northern Ireland is this architect-designed 10-metre-high wall which replaced a bare concrete blast wall around the RUC police station in Grosvenor Road, Belfast, in the mid-1980s.

create a no-go government citadel surrounded by a traffic-free *cordon sanitaire*. Unless terrorism abates altogether, further 'exclusion zones' will follow.

More heavily hit by terrorism than London has been the city of Belfast, the capital of Northern Ireland. There defensive measures are far more established. The years of sectarian violence going back to 1969, coupled with continuous peace-keeping operations by the military, have provided an unequalled training ground for planners to analyse the ways in which certain layouts facilitate terrorist attack, while others make it hard. In the same way the study of bombing incidents in Northern Ireland has showed how differently constructed buildings are affected by blast. Despite the fact that planning is not about aesthetics but about the quantity and location of development, while art-historical architecture is the reverse, each is resolutely drawn towards the territory of the other. In Northern Ireland the two have fused. Since the mid-1970s all major development projects there have had to be previewed and approved by the British Army.

In Belfast city centre closed-circuit surveillance cameras are everywhere. Shopping streets have turnstile-entry points and no unauthorized vehicle access is permitted. Like the constant monitoring of all vehicle movements around Northern Ireland, these measures are now so established that they occasion no more comment than the subtle changes in building layouts and approaches in the province. In Northern Ireland no new housing estate can be easily entered in a vehicle by one route and left by another. Except in a few old residential areas and where street patterns render it impossible, no carpark or access road can be found within 12 metres of an occupied building. In the same way the *real* entrance to any public or business building – its security checkpoint – is always 12 metres or more away from its 'architectural' entrance.

Within this uncongenial-sounding urban framework, the buildings themselves are also transformed. Their in-situ concrete or steel structural frames (no precast concrete work is permitted) are monolithic and coherent, designed to be self-supporting so that even if everything else falls down, they will still stand. Brick and concrete block infill panels, once the standby of commercial architecture in the province, are now shunned in favour of quickly replaceable plasterboard panels that will blow out and relieve the pressure of an explosion. Most obviously, large areas of glass, so common in the commercial architecture of London and all the world's major cities, are virtually non-existent.

One of the most obvious but least talked-about effects of terrorism, wherever it occurs, is the change it wreaks in the design and appearance of buildings, and what would be the consequences of change of this kind sustained over 50 or 100 years. Historic buildings were often designed with iron-barred windows that made it ostentatiously clear that they would be difficult to enter. Modern architecture on the other hand, with its emphasis on transparency and the merging of inside and outside space, dispensed with many of these traditional barriers. Nonetheless Modern and post-Modern architects design alike in that they use the traditional architectural elements – shape, shadow, line, fenestration, proportion, prospect and function. It is precisely when the terrorist threat becomes a matter of such overarching importance that the military security adviser becomes the lead consultant (instead of the architect), that these basic building blocks of design disappear and the police-post, the bunker and the pill-box take over. Then the whole process of design, root and branch, is revolutionized, as indeed is the idea of architecture as it has been known since the age of the fortified town and the walled city.

The first rule of security is to make the target inconspicuous, so any uniqueness of appearance or undue prominence in a building will immediately be ruled out. Urban addresses with clear numbering systems are discouraged, as are all terraced or semi-detached locations that allow access from neighbouring roofs. Instead of softening the lines and decorating the

London, July 1993, policemen laying out a road block. Following the explosion of the Bishopsgate bomb the government approved the introduction of temporary, then permanent road blocks around the City of London, as well as armed police patrols.

153

elevations of the buildings they surround, trees, shrubbery and climbing plants are kept well clear. Glass cladding for external walls is banned and transparency everywhere is removed by means of adhesive film or floor-to-ceiling splinter curtains. Windows in external walls are discouraged and courtyards or lightwells are preferred. Existing decorative features that might obstruct surveillance cameras are removed. All recesses, reveals and returns, undercrofts and stairs are deleted from the design, because they provide hiding places for bombs. Public access to atriums is denied, and subsidiary entrances and exits are permanently sealed up, as are basement carparks. Surface parking areas are sited as far away from the building as practicable.

The results of these and a hundred allied measures is to create an architecture so styleless that it can hardly be imagined. Its nondescript fortresses of serviced floorspace breathe freely only inside their own armoured carapace. In contemplating such structures our thoughts inevitably return to Charles Moore. Like prisons, such places will certainly help people know where they are and, by extension, who they are. But they may not like what they find.

8 The Urbanization of the Sand-heap

'There is a connection between urban breakdown and the lost cities of the past. The steps that lead to it are economic. What happens is that the people on the perimeter will never be able to afford to live within reach of the old central services. The rich, who can, will get richer and less numerous and the poor will be more numerous and get poorer. Thus the rich enclaves will start to be threatened with violence, robberies and anarchy. That will make the rich areas uninhabitable. There is a scenario. Twenty, forty, fifty years . . . It's heading for implosion.'

GLENN MURCUTT, 1995

Once upon a time all cities were megastructures, complex assemblies of spaces making the maximum use of shared structural walls, roofs and floors. The medieval city was like this, more like a nest of termites than a parade of palaces with boulevards and parks. In the medieval city there was virtually no public space, yet many mighty examples survived into the twentieth century without it: Venice, Teheran and Tokyo, to name but three. Some small towns like Gallipoli in Southern Italy, or Bonifacio in Corsica, are still practically devoid of open space today. So are the modern squatter settlements that have grown up around the capital cities of developing countries, and the refugee camps of the Middle East and Africa. Only a few great cities in the developed world, like Manhattan, Hong Kong or Singapore, have been forced to become megastructures because they have no space to expand into.

At the end of the twentieth century all surviving megastructures are special cases. Only injections of politics, luck and money have enabled them to continue to grow without soil, like hydroponic plants. But still they can teach us something. As we toddle like pygmies across the vast public spaces bequeathed to us by the urban planners of the nineteenth and twentieth centuries, we can reflect on the irresistible force of the decompression that was necessary to create such sprawling, unmanageable behemoths as Brasília, Los Angeles, Jacksonville, London or Paris. Had these cities

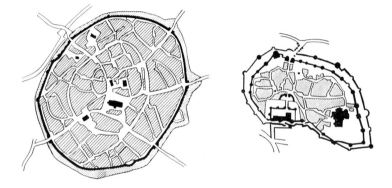

Medieval cities of the twelfth and thirteenth centuries show intense concentrations of development within man-made or natural defences. Few survive in their original form. Nordlingen, left, and Carcassonne (partially rebuilt in the nineteenth century) show high-density building and a minimum of public open space.

been walled in by politics for half a century – like Hong Kong or Singapore – they might have developed or, more correctly, re-developed, into high-rise megastructures.

Cities without suburbs and without public open space are potentially wealthy. High-intensity land use, especially on artificially created land, means that proportionally more investment is directed at less space. Servicing great vistas and detached buildings is different. It leads to increasing demands upon the public purse, so that maintenance alone becomes a burden, amortizing wealth and reducing the impact of investment.

Despite the synergetic advantages of concentration the long-term multifold trend in all cities is towards horizontal expansion and depopulation. In Europe this trend began centuries ago but was continually frustrated by warfare. It became stronger when the development of artillery reached the point where cities could no longer be defended by fixed fortifications, and finally overwhelmed all other considerations during the aerial bombardments of the Second World War, when urban evacuation became government policy in several combatant states.

In peacetime the construction of railways followed later by motor roads massively expanded the distances over which it was feasible to travel into the city every day. At the same time agronomy, refrigeration, world trade in foodstuffs and mechanized distribution removed the need for the urban hinterland to be used for food production and broke local supply links, making still more building land available in the process. By the middle of the twentieth century the only impediment to radical urban decentralization across the landscape was the slowness of provision of improved building land. It was while this problem was being addressed by means of the subsidized relocation of businesses and the construction of many regional shopping centres and town and village expansion schemes, that urban policy abruptly changed. Figures had showed that weakening of the employment base in the cities was leading to rising social costs, while falling tax revenues threatened the upkeep of transport infrastructure. Both were signs that the outward drift was beginning to drain the lifeblood of the city itself.

By the 1980s decentralization was no longer encouraged. Elaborate schemes brought forward in the 1960s to 'decant' inner-city dwellers to 'overspill' towns, as well as government

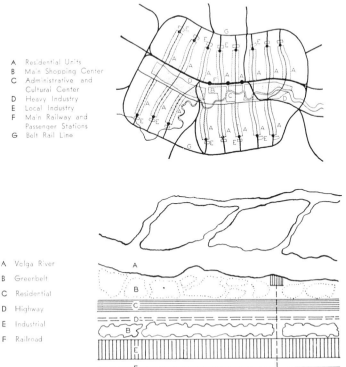

A   Residential Units
B   Main Shopping Center
C   Administrative and
      Cultural Center
D   Heavy Industry
E   Local Industry
F   Main Railway and
      Passenger Stations
G   Belt Rail Line

The 1930 Soviet plan for Stalingrad by N. A. Milyutin *(bottom)* and the 1944 MARS (Modern Architecture Research group) plan for London *(top)* show the same desire to reduce density.

A   Volga River
B   Greenbelt
C   Residential
D   Highway
E   Industrial
F   Railroad

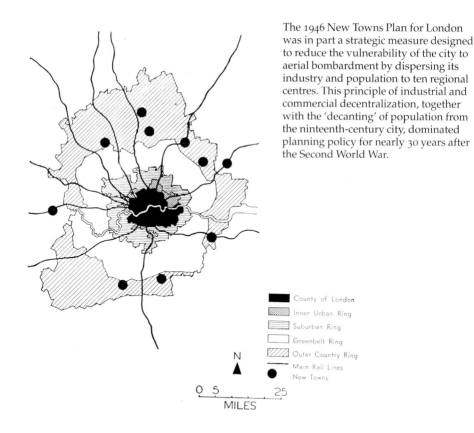

The 1946 New Towns Plan for London was in part a strategic measure designed to reduce the vulnerability of the city to aerial bombardment by dispersing its industry and population to ten regional centres. This principle of industrial and commercial decentralization, together with the 'decanting' of population from the ninteenth-century city, dominated planning policy for nearly 30 years after the Second World War.

County of London
Inner Urban Ring
Suburban Ring
Greenbelt Ring
Outer Country Ring
Main Rail Lines
New Towns

N

0 5   25
MILES

grants for employers prepared to 'relocate' in rural areas, were rapidly withdrawn. Land-use policies governing out-of-town retail and commercial developments were made more restrictive. But long before these new measures had even begun to come into effect their impact had already been neutralized by a new decentralizing force in the shape of dramatic improvements in communications technology. Computers linked to telecommunications networks began to threaten the whole concept of centrality. It was no longer a question of living in the country and working in town; offices themselves were threatening to become immaterial. For the vast majority of information-processing jobs it could be argued that it was hardly necessary to have an office at all. A cellular telephone, a car, a computer, a fax-modem and a cottage were all that was necessary to do business with half the world. In the 1990s government policy turned to the active discouragement of decentralization, which is where it stands today.

The financial crash of 1987, which in London followed only a year after the deregulation of the Stock Exchange, had already inflicted massive job losses. As a result, demand for office floorspace had dwindled and rents had begun to fall even as interest rates rose. Many property companies, highly geared to take advantage of the boom conditions immediately preceding the crash, faced cash-flow crises and went into receivership. By 1991, in the depths of a recession, it seemed entirely possible that the global information network, soon to be broadened yet further by tele-conferencing facilities, global satellite telephones and PC card data/fax modems, could halve office employment across the board and trigger a massive redundancy of commercial property from which there could be no recovery.

So apocalyptic was this prospect that the collapse of Communism and the triumph of the capitalist system, which was then a very recent event, began to look as though it might have been a photo finish. By 2000 at the latest it seemed that the gaudily patched-up 'treasure house' cities of the capitalist world, their property worthless, their tax base collapsing, would be heading for bankruptcy. It would never again be necessary to concentrate workers together in high-density business districts to make an economy work. In the tussle between 4,000 years of urban history and twenty years of microchip technology, it looked as though the tiny microchips were set to win hands down.

This preview of the ultimate urban crisis was not confined to Europe and the United States. Around the world there were other crowded cities, all eager to expand. As the Australian architect Glenn Murcutt put it in a 1995 interview:

> The fact that the computer is letting us link up with all over the world from a room in our house is going to make an immense difference to the way we operate in cities. It's going to break down urbanism as we've always understood it. It's going to reinforce suburbia and make the rural population able to survive much better than they ever survived before . . . Their biggest problem is the cost of transport to the cities. Once they ceased to have to do that, they could cut the cities off entirely and let them starve.[1]

Apart from vacuous boasting from city administrations themselves, claiming that a revival of prosperity and a massive investment in crumbling infrastructure was just around the corner, the only countervailing argument came from the veteran do-it-yourself urbanist Paolo Soleri (1919–). He theorized that cities could survive by following the pattern of miniaturization pioneered by the electronics industry itself. Soleri held out doggedly for urban concentration in a 1993 interview:

> In nature, as the organism evolves, it increases in complexity and also becomes more compact and miniaturized. The city too must become a more compact and miniaturized container for social, cultural and spiritual evolution. Nobody has ever understood that the megastructures we proposed at Arcosanti are in fact ministructures: that putting things together is a miniaturization, not a 'megaturization'. My solution is an urban implosion, rather than an explosion.[2]

It was true, a downsized city was theoretically just as feasible as a downsized radio or a downsized car. The electronics industry was downsizing its products all the time. Although Soleri did not claim this, the planned high density of his long-running Arcosanti project (a prototype city he and his volunteers have been building in the Arizona desert since the 1960s) was its greatest strength, a strength that could be traced back a thousand years to the urban megastructures of the Middle Ages and the Mediterranean tradition.

But the fact remained that human beings could not be downsized. Pre-industrial compactness had not guaranteed the survival of cities in the past. With exceptions that could be counted on the fingers of one hand, the story of twentieth-century urbanism had been decentralization from beginning to end. Now new technology had broken the egg of the old city and threatened to spill its contents all over the landscape.

All that this promised was urban destruction, slower than the catastrophes of history but just as sure. And the roll call of urban disasters in history was endless. There was Mycenae and Jerash, Carthage, Palmyra and Pompeii. Only a little over 300 years ago London had been half destroyed by fire and Lisbon levelled by an earthquake. In our own century urban destruction had been industrialized by artillery and bombing. Rotterdam had been bombed; Lübeck and Nuremberg had been burned and Exeter, Bath and York bombed in reprisal.

Eight square miles of Hamburg had been destroyed by fire-storm; Warsaw had been razed to the ground; and sixteen square miles of Tokyo and six square miles of Hiroshima and Nagasaki had been utterly destroyed.

More recent still was the ghastly fate of Saigon during the Vietnam War. Ronald Spector's account in *After Tet* conveys the horror of twentieth-century disurbanization even though he is not describing the final collapse of 1972 but only the state of the city after the Viet Cong offensive of 1968. Saigon's population was then 3 million, twice what it had been five years before. In addition to the indigenous population there were 500 squatters living on every acre of urban land. The incidence of cholera, smallpox, bubonic plague and typhoid was higher than in any other world city. Children born in Saigon had only one chance in three of reaching the age of four. The city lived on petroleum, with 100,000 motorcycles, 25,000 motor scooters, 25,000 trucks and more than 400,000 bicycles and pedicabs, making a total of more than 2,700 civilian vehicles for every mile of road. There were innumerable bars and 56,000 registered prostitutes. Garbage piled up in the streets until the stacks were half a block long. After the Tet offensive the scale of Viet Cong terrorist attacks within the city, combined with the military measures used to suppress them, make the IRA's efforts against the City of London in the 1990s – and the City of London's defences against the IRA – pale into insignificance. In Saigon in May 1968 no less than 87,000 people were made homeless by ground or air attacks by friendly forces in response to terrorist bombing and sniping. The much-publicized 'New Life Construction Project', a massive 80-acre, five-year, demonstration low-cost, self-build housing project financed by the South Vietnamese government, was totally destroyed in two days. And all the while guests at the high-rise Caravel Hotel in the centre of the city, vying for seats in the top-floor restaurant to eat steak and lobster, watched while helicopter gun-ships and ground-attack aircraft went to work on the outlying suburbs.

It may seem far-fetched to evoke such a catastrophe, the consequence of an appalling war, in connection with a still hypothetical urban crisis born of the decentralizing effect of electronic signals, satellite echoes, groaning faxes, cellular phones and rows of digits on monitor screens. But in a world that is growing megacities of 15 or 20 million people, a world where, as the architect Rem Koolhaas has said, 'urbanism has stopped, but urbanization goes on', there is much fear surrounding the process. According to the 1997 report of the Asian Development Bank[3] the number of Asian cities with populations exceeding 10 million is expected to rise from nine to twenty by 2025. But to provide them with effective urban infrastructure will require investment of the order of $40 billion a year for the next ten years. Short of this high level of investment, the bank predicts, they will be overwhelmed by pollution, congestion, crime and social dislocation as well as flooding and salination from groundwater depletion. Glenn Murcutt takes a similarly pessimistic view:

> Technically, theoretically, there should be a solution for the Asian city states like Hong Kong and Singapore because they are so concentrated. There should be a kind of efficiency in that, but so far it always seems to remain theoretical. The intensity of waste generated by those cities takes oceans and hemispheres to dispose of.[4]

Fear of the dislocation of urban services on a massive scale is endemic in the populations of all great cities, not only in Asia but in Europe and the Americas. The larger the city, the more deep-seated the fear that one day it will fail. As history shows, such fears cannot be dismissed. All intimations of urban disaster are plausible, and most have happened before, from those that begin with power cuts and packed subway trains stalled in deep tunnels, to those that involve fire, epidemics of disease or outbreaks of war. It may be a reflection of these fears that, while all the modern cities that were destroyed in the Second World War have since been rebuilt, every one, including finally Berlin, has been reduced in density in the process.

In any event the catalogue of the urban disintegrations of the past is not confined to natural and military disasters. The 'rationalization' of Paris by Baron Haussmann was a form of megastructural demolition; so was Benito Mussolini's 'disencumberment' of the surviving monuments of ancient Rome, likewise the motor roads driven through the urban fabric of Teheran in the 1930s. More recent still has been the pernicious effect of the preservation of larger and larger sections of cities as conservation areas, where time virtually stands still. The great urbanist Spiro Kostof saw this well-meant halting of urban evolution as as great a danger as war or pestilence. In *The City Assembled* he insisted that living cities were never truly still. 'If the city is to survive,' he wrote, 'process must have the final word. In the end urban truth is in the flow.'

Albert Einstein, the endorser of the theories of Richard Buckminster Fuller and Le Corbusier,[5] taught the world that the connection between space and time is not remote. Nor is it complicated, for it can be demonstrated by the operation of an ordinary camera. Under given conditions of light, time values are inversely proportional to aperture values in the exposure of film. The faster the shutter of the camera moves, the larger the aperture required to correctly expose the film, and vice versa. Applying the principle of the relativity of time and space in a camera to time and space in a city, produces a useful theorem. If urban space is equated with aperture size, and urban time with shutter speed, the less space a city possesses, the more time it has available. Conversely the more space it has, the less time.

If urban events were to become instantaneous, as they would if continuous on-line communications encompassed the world day and night, then urban space might dwindle to nearly nothing. There would be no need for urban space as we understand it today. The whole world's population could be in a state of global awareness through a network of four billion tubes 300 atoms in diameter – the 'aperture size' of the beam of light that will be required by tomorrow's optical computer systems.

There is another more prosaic way of looking at the space/time continuum in cities. Consider the crossroads, the street-level four-way intersection that has been a feature of the urban plan for thousands of years and in one form or another survives in every city today. Over the centuries, as traffic speeds and densities have increased, it has evolved into a controlled intersection. Now, by means of robot coloured lights, it is an automatically controlled intersection. But even in its ultimate form, with right and left filter lights, pedestrian crossing intervals and computer-phased sequencing, its traffic capacity is still tiny because its 'aperture' is fixed. Because it is two-dimensional, only four vehicle directions at most – as opposed to the theoretical twelve – can be used at any one time. By contrast a two-dimensional four-way traffic intersection in an optical system has no difficulty in accepting traffic in all twelve directions simultaneously. The 'vehicles' pass through one another by the simple expedient of varying the optical wavelength or the colour of the light beams on which they travel. Not only can all twelve directions be in use all the time, but a three-dimensional intersection can be constructed so that traffic in 144 directions can be accommodated simultaneously. This is a hard point to grasp. What it means is that, whereas the traffic throughput of a conventional urban street system is limited by the number and complexity of its intersections, the 'traffic' through an optical system is completely unaffected by them. An optical city would operate at such speed that it would have infinite space. Conceptually it could encompass the globe, or even the universe. Its 'streets' could be millions of miles long, its individual buildings mere atoms, like cobblestones.

And this of course is what is beginning to take shape today. It is the opening scene in the great urban explosion that is taking place in our own time. Citizens feel as though they are dwindling to the size of pygmies while their states of

The advent of an enlarged European Community in the 1980s created the possibility of regional planning on a trans-national scale. Here two urban zones, the 'Dorsale', reaching from Manchester in the north almost to Rome, and a smaller zone dependent on Paris, hint at even lower-density development in the future.

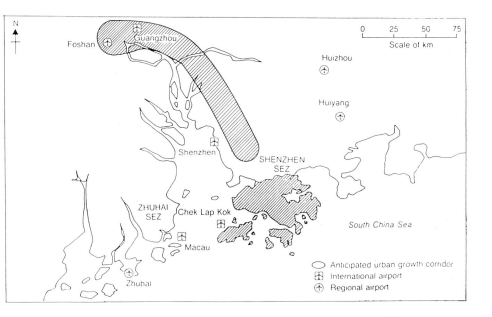

Foshan · Guangzhou

Huizhou ⊕

Huiyang ⊕

Shenzhen

SHENZHEN SEZ

ZHUHAI SEZ · Chek Lap Kok

Macau

Zhuhai

South China Sea

0   25   50   75
Scale of km

◯ Anticipated urban growth corridor
⊞ International airport
⊕ Regional airport

N

An Asian equivalent to the 'Dorsale' is the Pearl River delta urban zone in China. Reaching in a 250-kilometre arc from Guangzhou to Shenzhen and ultimately to Hong Kong, its outline is already traced by airports, a modern motorway and improved rail links.

communication, which are the 'cities' that they really live in, are growing to infinite size, far beyond the power of any urban administration to control. It is as though the environment they have lived in for years has suddenly been magnified one million times while they, its former masters, have become no more than atoms within it.

In his 1991 essay 'Three Times', Vilém Flusser, the Czechoslovak media philosopher, described the sequential evolution of three different types of time.[6] The first of these he called 'wheel time', a cyclical time that found its origins in the seasonal and generational patterns of the agrarian, pre-industrial world. Next came linear or 'stream time', which flowed from the past to the future by way of progress and increasing mastery over the natural world. This was the idea of time that governed the Modern Age, the age of exploration and discovery that brought forth great advances in science and industry. But Vilém Flusser was a post-Modern thinker. His third conception of time went beyond the forward-looking belief in progress of the Modern Age to a state of inertia that he called 'sand-heap time'. It is a concept which, like the optical intersection, has a crucial relevance to the shape of the post-urban future.

Flusser visualized 'sand-heap time' as a time of uniformly

165

distributed particles whose events are neither cyclical, as in 'wheel time', nor linear, as in 'stream time'. 'Sand-heap time' neither rotates nor progresses: its activity is entirely entropic. It gradually erodes away all kinetic gradients until all that is left is an inert, uniform layer, like sand upon a beach.

A good parallel for the transition from 'stream time' to 'sand-heap time' might be the industrial process that involves the breaking-up of a treated silicon wafer, only 0.25mm thick, into hundreds of tiny microchips. The wafer starts out as the object of a linear production process, but once it is broken into microchips its elements have no further connection with one another except the uniformity of their destination, which is somewhere in the global infrastructure of information processing. After the parent wafer is broken, each chip, like a grain of sand, becomes one of a million inert events on their way to eventlessness.

'Sand-heap time' is the corollary of our new world of instantaneous global presence, the appropriate measure of time for a universe in which satellite communications have made the concept of physical travelling speed as meaningless as it was thousands of years ago, when mankind could only walk. But by the analogy of the camera, instantaneous speed must also mean infinite space, and it is in the relationship between these two absolutes, on the brink of attainment for the first time in human history, that 'sand-heap urbanism' comes into being as the correct image of an inert, evenly distributed network of settlements utterly without physical movement. 'Sand-heap urbanism' is the name of the post-urban, post-art-historical pattern of life-support terminals that will be the built environment of the next century but one. In the age of 'sand-heap urbanism' there will not be world cities, but a world of cities. There will be a resolution of the apparently irreconcilable contradiction between concentration and dispersal in the shape of the final destruction of the traditional model of the megastructure.

Images of what Vilém Flusser meant by 'sand-heap time' – realized through such analogies as the camera, the traffic intersection and the breaking of a silicon wafer – make it possible to see that neither the reformation of the city into a miniaturized, high-density version of itself, nor a cataclysmic exodus of its population, is necessary to bring 'sand-heap urbanism' about. Like an undetected cancer, its primary

Part of a new 'stealth' rural settlement dependent on satellite communications and concealed supply networks (Image by Nigel Gilbert).

cause must have been something in the urban past that began demolishing parts of the city centuries ago and slowly metastased into every part of it, long before its contemporary economic vulnerability was recognized.

Where were the clues to this sickness? They were everywhere, carefully hidden, as if by a superior intelligence, in areas where no cumulative effect was suspected. Within the city itself contributory transformations continue to take place before our eyes, as they always have in the past. Former royal palaces and government offices become hotels, museums or art galleries. Great military barracks disappear. Warehouses become apartments and docks become airports. Once-logical street patterns become incoherent and counter-intuitive as a result of one-way systems and pedestrianized areas. To an astonishing extent in the years since the Second World War a 'replacement city' has occupied the dead bodies of most of the great cities left over from history.

Tourism provides a paradigm for the clandestine arrival of 'sand-heap urbanism'. As fast as the old producer functions desert the metropolis, its working population melts away with them. But at the same time, this genuine loss of 'factual' population is masked by the arrival of a growing 'fictional' population of tourists. Today London has an immense fictional population of this kind, as do other world cities. Of the 26 million overseas visitors who came to Britain in 1996, half never left London. In effect the city welcomes double its native population in visitors every year, and at peak vacation times nearly half its population consists of 'fictional' visitors from overseas.

Tourists look like citizens, many even look like residents,

A pedestrianized street in Covent Garden, London. The banning of traffic from thoroughfares leads to immense gatherings of tourists, creating the impression of a population density that does not really exist.

ready to defend old urban values, but they are not. They are phantoms whose unwitting role is to change the nature of urbanism by deception. Their presence disguises the flight of commerce and industry, both of which have left the city centre forever. Tourists are a form of camouflage that hides urban emptiness, yet to accommodate them traffic lanes are lost to coach parking, historic traffic routes are closed to vehicles, and public open spaces are extended by pedestrianization – all measures that simultaneously accelerate the disappearance of the old producer economy. Such disruptions to commerce as speed bumps, gated roads, bus lanes and cycle paths, which would never have been countenanced by municipal authorities even 30 years ago, are welcomed. Few recognize them for what they are, annexations of public rights of way by an 'industry' that displaces trade, pays no rent and destroys the circuit boards of the urban economy like a virus.

Today tourism exerts enormous influence over urban policy. In Britain it has prompted government measures to expel beggars from city streets – as a result of opinion polls that show that a high percentage of foreign visitors are disturbed by their presence. The introduction to the 1997 edition of the *Official Handbook of Britain*, an annual publication which is widely used as a reference work by the British Council overseas, expresses official approval for the encouragement of wealthy tourists and the discouragement of poorer ones: 'One high-spending US tourist outweighs a coach full of day-trippers from across the Channel arriving with packed lunches and an itinerary of free attractions who merely clog up the streets and end up costing the country more money than they bring in.'[7] And indeed, it could be added, creates far less traffic congestion than the thousands of tour buses that render the operations of surface public transport more and more difficult.

Though its significance is always underrated, tourism is not the only hidden agent of urban change. Over the years most of the buildings lining the streets of the old producer cities have been clandestinely rebuilt in the form of consumer envelopes, with fewer and fewer producer elements, even though their visible architecture does not reflect this change. This is because urban architecture is becoming more and more a 'fictional' construct itself. Over the twenty years since the closure of London's docks and the end of industry and administration in the capital, London has seen an end to public housing, an end to investment in roads and an end to unrestricted vehicular ownership. During the same period 'stealth architecture' has arrived, the variant of post-Modern architecture described in the last chapter that is specially designed to retain reassuringly undisturbed historic façades.

This widespread architectural deception is an infrastructural equivalent to the phantom population generated by tourism. It too operates as a camouflage to conceal the fact that the real operations of the economy are increasingly moving out of the city. Figures released by the National Audit Office in 1997 indicate that the amount of unused government office floorspace in London, held on long leases from property companies, doubled between 1992 and 1996, reaching 400,000 square metres. For Britain as a whole the total reached 830,000 square metres, half as big again as the entire projected development of Canary Wharf.[8] During the same period corporate spending on information technology in the City of London rose from £1.3 billion to £2.5 billion and was projected to rise to £4 billion by 2000.[9] Neither empty offices nor new communications installations advertise their connection to outsiders. Nor do 'stealth buildings' or 'filmable façades'. But putting them all together is not difficult. For obvious reasons airline and airport magazines have no problem with the concept: 'The bigger the city, the bigger the cost advantage of avoiding it and getting the people together at the airport instead.'[10]

169

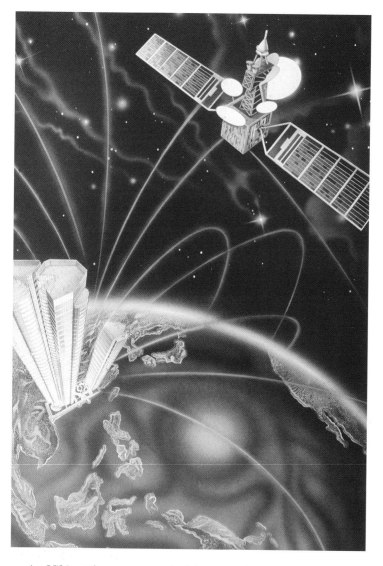

Satellite communications as visualized in Hong Kong.

As Vilém Flusser wrote in his essay 'Line and Surface',[11] there used only to be two kinds of medium in the world of facts: linear media, like writing, which presented them in a historical succession so that they illustrated a process; and surface media, like architecture, which presented them statically, in scenes. In our own time a third type of medium has come into existence, a medium that converts the fact of a building into the fiction of the thin film of its façade. It is this film that the audience of tourists watches when imbibing their fictional version of the city. Internally the function of commercial buildings has been robotized by information technology, but it does not show. As Toyo Ito explains:

> People and cars are no longer the only moving objects in our cities. The flow of diverse forms of energy and information is increasing at a tremendous rate, and indeed the flow of such invisible things is beginning to dominate urban space. Yet we cannot conjure up an architectural image of an information space because information does not give rise to a physical form.[12]

In an extreme case of 'stealth building', like Nomura International, the disembowelment of the four original façades is less important than the unknown meaning of these new internal organs. The result of such heroic surgery, which eagerly collaborates with the force of electronically annihilated distance, is that all formerly real places and all formerly recognizable categories of building are disappearing. Their 'historical strata' have been compressed like computer files. By such means the contemporary city conceals the manner in which urban real estate is already fighting for its life. 'Stealth buildings', heritage façades, fast-track construction, skilful project management, design-and-build contracting, better climate controls, more information technology, ruthless value engineering and better exit strategies have so far kept property values afloat – just – but the worst impact of the information revolution is still to come.

Translated into a spatial concept, 'sand-heap time' becomes 'sand-heap urbanism', the product of the grand urban deceptions wrought by tourism, 'stealth architecture' and telepresence. In this new guise it represents the key to the redefinition of urbanity as an instantaneously timed, infinitely apertured, omnidirectional phenomenon. Instead of clinging disastrously to the profitless merry-go-round of subsidized 'cultural' consumption, this new urbanism works by configuration instead of movement. Its public open space is a vast and scaleless global network that is neither metropolis nor wilderness but infinity: something that is willing itself into existence with a remorselessness untouched by human plan. This immensely powerful force is recognized by Paolo Soleri but spurned by him because of the very formlessness that is its strength:

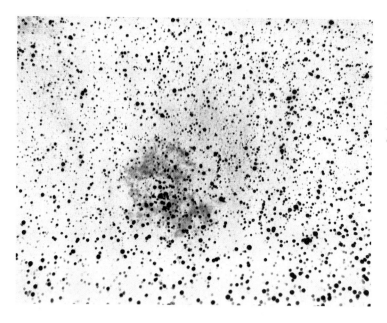

Part of a Rosette Nebula in the galaxy of monoceros visualized as a dispersed network of habitations overlaid upon the remains of an abandoned high-density settlement.

Urban megastructures used to be considered the worst thing possible because they were confused with suburbia, which is not a structure at all, not an organism, not even a system. Suburbia doesn't work because it is endless matter which is flat, amorphic and tenuous. It promises so much but it gives so little.[13]

Soleri sees the significance of suburbia, but he does not accept it. Similarly, it must be said, Vilém Flusser seemed unwilling to follow the logic of his own final form of time. For him 'sand-heap time' was entropy, the end of everything, something to be fought every inch of the way. Yet suburbia, entropy and 'sand-heap urbanism' all belong to the same process. In their different ways they are the measure of our progress towards the solid state universe of inert particles that is the destination of all our planning, design and construction. When Soleri dismisses suburbia, and Flusser rejects entropy, each of them does less than justice to their own insight.

In his study of the thermodynamics of man-made and natural ecologies, *Environment, Power and Society*, Howard Odum drew a distinction between 'connected associations' dependent on strong power flows, such as reefs of oysters, heavy root networks in tropical rain forests and contiguous urban structuring in cities, and 'unconnected associations', or entropies, without strong power flows, like the organisms in plankton in the sea, scattered plants in a newly sown field, or suburban housing. Odum saw a similarity between modern cities and 'concentrations of consumers' among seabed creatures such as oysters, clams and barnacles, all of which rely upon strong power inflows to bring energy and oxygen, and strong outflows to dispose of heat and waste. From his studies of renewal and decay in the habitat of both kinds of 'concentrations of consumers', Odum concluded that monolithic rigid structures akin to cities only emerged where power flows were highly concentrated, and that in all cases the power needed increased in direct proportion to the size of the structure to be maintained. Odum's analysis went on:

> Only connected associations develop senescence at the group level as well as within individuals. We are used to the idea in urban renewal that some continuous building structures are more cheaply replaced than repaired. An example in a simple ecosystem is the senescence of barnacle associations. When old and top-heavy they break off or are broken off and new growth and succession refills the gaps.[14]

The important thing about Odum's research is that it suggests an explanation for the remorseless spread of cities in a language that is neither art-historical nor political but structural. In this way it can be much more closely related to the entropic implications of 'sand-heap urbanism'.

Odum's ecological perspective shows us that when space occurs in one of his non-human concentrations of consumers it is not a cultural phenomenon but a gap. It has no reproduction or survival function. In the natural associations that he studied, gaps occurred through aged structures disintegrating or by accidental damage. Wherever possible they were repaired by the organisms by accretion into the surviving mass. This was done because accretive construction minimizes effort and possesses synergetic strength advantages. Gap repair was a continuous process that eventually overwhelmed the capabilities of the organisms. Gaps that outweighed the mass of the remainder of the structure were always problematic. Too many gaps and the natural megastructure broke down entirely and its constituent fragments were dispersed.

Comparisons of the quantum of work involved in repairs versus new construction in human settlements suggest that it is at least analogically possible to argue that urban space in long-established cities also originated as 'gap' space – evidence of damage or want of resources for repair rather than the outcome of planning and design. As far as we can judge today, medieval cities, like connected associations of molluscs (or today's contemporary squatter settlements and distribution parks), always started out as 'concentrations of consumers' without gaps. What is most striking about the medieval towns and cities that survive is their almost total lack of public open space. What is most striking about later perimeter development is the proliferation of gaps, becoming larger and larger as the distance from the centre increases.

For the most part it was not until the nineteenth century that the incorporation of large public open spaces into city plans came to be seen as a public good, and even then it arose as a means of coping with the demolition of old fortifications, the consequence of great fires and natural disasters, or the damage caused by wars and revolutions. In effect all such open spaces were originally gaps in a megastructure that could not be filled. The buildings and vistas, parks and gardens, that were laid out across these 'gaps' in later years were soon rationalized into elements of urban planning, but only after the collapse of the 'gap-filling' capability of the original, megastructural idea.

Given the dramatic extent to which 'gap repair' has failed to keep pace with suburban dilution in the twentieth century, we must conclude either that our cities are progressively de-densifying themselves, or that some form of non-architectural 'gap repair' is actually taking place, but that it is not visible to urban planners because it does not consist of buildings, vistas or monuments and has little or no capital value. In effect both these conclusions are true. Cities are losing density, but this loss is more and more connected with the tightening grip of the non-place-specific networks of information that now link all cities and non-cities into an endless global continuum.

The settlement pattern that will result is the circuit diagram of 'sand-heap urbanism'. It represents the ideal physical distribution of humanity into insignificant, undifferentiated, uniformly distributed particles without urban space, without

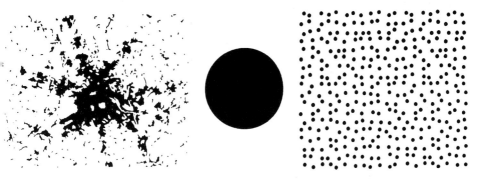

Comparative distributions of identical populations. Left, the built-up area of the city of Berlin as it presently exists. Centre, the same built-up area at the level of concentration of a medieval megastructure. Right, an undifferentiated distribution of the same population with no concentrations – in effect a 'sand-heap' disurbanization.

urban identity, without heritage, without history. All we have to do to conform to the directive of 'sand-heap urbanism' is to continue to leak away the old wealth of our cities into instantaneous electronic awareness. It is the blueprint for the global information network by which all individuals will be in all cities, and all cities will be a single city of the world.

Today the urban future is on pause, awaiting the fall of producer reality and the triumph of consumer reality. Producer reality is tied to place; consumer reality lives in space. During this hiatus its citizens live in both place and space: leading a privatized existence that combines the factitious danger and inconvenience of urban life with the eerie out-of-body experience of electronic global awareness. For them the permanent architectural constructs of the city represent the 'primary reality' of place, while the transient episodes of global awareness achieved through cinema, video, TV and music amount to a 'secondary reality' that is experienced as time out of time. This is as unstable a state collectively as it is individually. Urban populations are fragmented, collectively and individually, their brains riddled with a confusing mixture of local experience and global information. As a result they become less and less like residents (indigenous producers) and more and more like visitors (touristical consumers). As the crisis of urban real estate approaches, critical mass is steadily moving from resident status to visitor status. Already, to act out these two roles simultaneously requires every urban individual to have, in effect, two bodies: a 'factual' primary reality body consisting of his or her tangible physical presence, and a 'fictional' secondary reality body shaped by the information space it commands. Inevitably, as the city becomes more and more consumerized, this second 'fictional' body becomes more and more demanding. Soon its growth and expansion will dissolve all traditional 'factual' relationships. All close-proximity place-based relationships, community, employment, family, kinship, marriage, cohabitation . . . every link dependent on interdependence and place will give way to an equivalent time-based 'fictional' consumer relationship. Reflecting and conforming to this change, the very architecture of the city will be compelled to lose its factual producer identity and dissolve into discontinuous hotel-style, time-based consumer accommodation – a process that can already be seen at work in the conversion of superfluous office buildings into apartments. In the end the city of 'fictional' consumers will no longer require a resident producer population, except in the sense that a theme park requires uniformed staff and security guards. These trained 'consumption consultants' will represent all that is left of the great producer populations of the industrial cities of the nineteenth and early twentieth centuries and the pre-industrial medieval craft cities before that. By the standards of history the 'factual producer' populations of our cities have already ceased to exist. As we have seen in previous chapters, their absence is masked by the presentation of dramatized media communities, 'stealth architecture' and a growing 'fictional' population of tourists.

We can pursue the fate of the 'fictional' consumer only one step further before he or she is buried in the non-fiction of contemporary life. A case in point is the paradigm for the operation of a future urban 'hotel apartment' offered by the phenomenon of Home Parenteral Nutrition or HPN. This is a type of intravenous nutrition therapy that is available to sufferers from internal disorders that prevent the digestion of nutrients by normal means. Using HPN, sufferers from visceral myopathy can live at home and be fed while they sleep by means of a feed bag whose contents are infused via an administration set which connects the bag via a catheter to a central line surgically placed in a vein. Explaining that HPN costs between £25,000 and £43,000 a year, the journal *Medical Interface* describes the administrative process as follows:

> When there is no longer any reason for the patient to stay in hospital apart from his or her feed, we explain the situation, contact their GP, and then contact the purchasing authority, to explain that the patient will need TPN to sustain him or her for life. We explain that we can put a package together and see if they accept it. This consists of the feeding regimen, all the disposables he or she will need and the capital cost items – the pump, the stand, the trolley and the fridge.[15]

At the time of writing there is a relatively small constituency for HPN and TPN (Total Parenteral Nutrition), but a 350-member patient group exists in Britain and there are much larger organizations in the United States and Canada. A 'civilian' development of HPN is one way in which urban consumers could increase the balance of their 'time out of time' experience at the expense of producer activity in the future. This shift would be multiplied by the added ingredient of reality-simulation as envisioned in Chapter 1 and discussed at some length in Chapter 2.

It is the fate of the old city to disintegrate. We believe it because the privileged macroscopic truth of the twentieth century, the truth that we see from the air that is denied on the ground, shows us that what seems at ground level to be urban growth and expansion is in reality urban dispersal. Planning changes nothing. The counter-entropic striving for development control leads ultimately to a built environment that requires no development control. That is why in the nineteenth century the suburbs were born. In the twenty-first century the uncontrolled zone is the information city of global electronic awareness. The invisible city is prefigured, as William Southwood has pointed out, by the telephone system: 'The largest single machine ever constructed and probably the most important'.[16]

It is the fate of architecture in this invisible global city to ephemeralize. For like dispersal, ephemeralization is a resultant force. It is the end product of a process of species selection brought about by an environment that is more and more informationalized. Urban dispersal multiplied by information technology means terminal architecture.

9 Terminal Architecture

'The meaning of the message is the change it produces in the image.'
MARSHALL McLUHAN, 1964

When the staff of a merchant bank in the City of London go home at the end of the day, the firm's computers do not rest. Instead they kick in to a special programme that sets them to work downloading the day's business onto a data recorder in a vault somewhere miles away. This is part of a prearranged plan. Another part of it will come into operation should the firm's City offices be bombed, set on fire, flooded or otherwise disabled before opening for business the following morning. In such a case key staff will be telephoned automatically and advised to rendezvous at a different address, probably in a nondescript, hard-to-let building on the outskirts of London. Wherever it is, this so-called 'hot site' will already be equipped with workstations, personal computers, telephone lines and data terminals. Essential staff will work from this location until the difficulty at the main office has been resolved.

Ever since the first big IRA bomb attacks on the City of London in 1993 and 1994, every major financial institution in London has availed itself of these unobtrusive 'business continuity services'. Initially several accepted downloading vaults in Docklands, but this location lost favour after one or two were damaged by the Canary Wharf bomb of February 1996. Nowadays more remote locations are preferred. There is no requirement for a 'hot site' to be a special kind of building or to be protected from terrorist attack itself. It is a data warehouse, an expendable and interchangeable facility. Virtually everything to do with its usefulness relates to the needs of information processing, for as the complexity and importance of information technology increases, so does the security problem it poses to business.

Defects in buildings, up to and including their destruction by fire or high explosives, are trivial matters by comparison with computer down-time. In 1997 the property agents Savills estimated that for a medium-sized office in the City, the loss of a single day's business through computer disruption is about £100,000. A single day of disruption across the whole United Kingdom could cost £1.4 billion. Figures of this order explain why, important as they are in computer terms, 'hot site' buildings have no status as architecture. Ideally they are run-down premises without distinguishing features of any kind. Perhaps the worst fate for any of them would be to be declared to be of special architectural or historical interest. To become a Listed building would be a sentence of death. They are information terminals, pure and simple.

Damage caused by the February 1996 terrorist bomb exploded in London's Docklands.

In 1987 there were no companies in Britain offering 'business continuity services'; in 1997 there were more than 40. Today these companies provide automatic data recording facilities, remote office lettings and emergency network planning. Born in the wake of terrorist activities in several countries, the earliest firms in the field called themselves 'disaster recovery organizations'. Nowadays the less inflammatory title is preferred, not only because it too is inconspicuous, but because bombings and fires are relatively rare. Computer system failures, thefts and employee sabotage are much more common. A 1997 report[1] estimated that full business continuity services, covering all risks from bombs to staff sickness, cost companies £5,000 a year for every workstation insured. Sources estimate the total expenditure to be over £50 million a year.

It is a measure of the transformation that has taken place in the relative status of place, space and information that 'business continuity plans', automatic computer records and 'hot site' offices are now considered to be as vital to business as were the same kind of facilities to the command networks of the military forces of the Cold War. At the dawn of the twenty-first century, 'business continuity', following in the footsteps of the identity badge, the access code and the security guard, has completed a migration from the military to the civilian sphere: a migration that confirms the magnified importance of business intelligence in a competitive world with few captive markets, and underlines its new, quasi-military character.

This transformation has already exhibited remarkable side effects. Not least the fact that, in corporate terms, security is now far more important, and far more expensive, than architecture. Indeed architecture, particularly conspicuous, lavish and creative architecture, has become a business liability. The grand corporate headquarters is an inviting target for terrorists and protest groups, or for any individual with a grudge. Along with corporate downsizing and dispersal, this reasoning has played an important part in the evacuation of central London by such major entities as Shell and IBM. Nor is this a national issue. The same thinking operates in the United States where, for example the new Dallas Exxon headquarters, designed by Hellmuth Obata and Kassabaum and completed in 1996, is not only located on an out-of-town site but is subject to an absolute publication and video embargo. Pursuing the same logic other major corporations not only equip themselves with 'hot sites' but acquire 'remote sites' too, turning these into the centres where their core business is transacted. The German airline Lufthansa, for example, has shopfront offices in major cities all over the world, but its reservations are handled from a 'call centre' in Galway in Ireland – as are those of American Airlines and Korean Air.

Camouflaged by its inconspicuousness, the 'hot site' is a paradigm for Terminal Architecture. Under the impact of information technology and the new media, all buildings, from the private dwelling to the mighty office tower, are beginning to slip away from the art-historical realm of permanent and appreciating value into a limbo where their real value resides in their rock-bottom information utility alone. In his later years Howard Hughes, the reclusive American billionaire, eschewed his corporate limousine in favour of an old Chevrolet in order not to attract attention. He was a precursor. Today experts in the art of fitting organizations into buildings are also beginning to relish the inconspicuous, the remote and the neglected.

To most people the kind of architecture that will dominate the twenty-first century remains a mystery. It is as though we believe, perhaps even hope, that the remaining minutes of the twentieth century will still hold a surprise or two in store. This is a strange idea. Nothing can be built in sufficient quantity between now and the Millennium to transform the imprint of our century and turn it into something else. The average life of our buildings is so long that not only is the identity of the twentieth century ineradicable, but the image of the twenty-first is already clear. Just as the buildings of the Victorian era set the agenda for the Modern Age, so have the buildings of the New Elizabethans set the agenda for the post-Modern. The canonical buildings of England in the twentieth century are few. Only a handful have passed into the public consciousness – the Royal Festival Hall, Coventry Cathedral, the Lloyds building, the Sainsbury Wing of the National Gallery, Stansted Airport terminal, the Canary Wharf Tower, but not many more. What really sets the stage for the twenty-first century is another kind of building altogether, a type so large, so numerous and so anonymous that it does not appear on ordnance survey maps, is not kept up to date by aerial photographic surveys, and is in all other respects almost completely ignored.

Today Large Single-Storey Buildings or LSSBs, better known as 'Big Sheds', can be found all over the British Isles, everywhere except in the centres of our towns and cities. Exiled from metropolitan sites, they cluster instead on poor-quality land and disused airfields close to the 150 numbered exits and interchanges of 1,800 miles of motorway where they constitute a kind of non-residential urbanism that has no historical precedent. Not only are these 'Big Sheds' of unexampled size and simplicity of appearance but, because no one ever built on the sites they occupy before the second half of the twentieth century, their planning is unconstrained by historic precedent. Indeed, their anonymity goes so far that less than half of the local authority structure plans in England indicate the location of any out-of-town distribution centre, even though up to one third of the new serviced floorspace completed every year consists of new distribution centres.

A good place to contemplate 'Big Shed' town planning is 130 miles west of London, where the M5 motorway crosses the River Avon close to the docks at Avonmouth. There, at Portbury, is one of the most impressive distribution complexes in Britain. Although they do not know it, the thousands who head this way to holiday in the West Country each summer pass the architecture of the twenty-first century, already in place, years ahead of its time.

Portbury is a showplace of Terminal Architecture, with nondescript but dramatic buildings set next to quays as long as airport runways, ships as big as blocks of flats, deep basins, wide roads, narrow tracks, old military huts, new bungalows and, most of all, enormous 'Big Sheds' strewn around like a child's building blocks after a cosmic tantrum.

Generally speaking, LSSBs are steel-framed buildings with laser-flat concrete floors, and walls and roofs formed from sandwich panels with pre-finished inner and outer skins. These steel- and aluminium-skinned rectangles are the wholesale granaries of consumer society, filled to bursting with immense stocks of every kind of merchandise, from toys and games to refrigerated groceries. Served by fleets of articulated trucks, their massive, featureless exteriors defy the terminology of conventional twentieth-century architectural

Building where no one had ever built before. This aerial photograph of Portbury, near Bristol, shows the emergence of a new 'Big Shed' landscape in the Gordano Valley. Centred on the new docks and the M5 motorway, the shape of this development is overlaid upon the patchwork of fields in the same way as the fields were once overlaid upon primeval forest.

A pioneer computerized distribution centre at Birtley, near Newcastle-upon-Tyne, designed by CWS Architects' Department and completed in 1970. One of the first attempts at automated mechanical handling in Britain, it came into operation in 1971 and replaced 50 smaller urban warehouses.

criticism. Like the 'stealth buildings' of the city, 'Big Sheds' leave everything to the imagination. Their names – typically Argos, Asda, Tesco, Waitrose, Makro – are the names of superstores, but they are not public access buildings. Most of them are giant windowless rectangular boxes, 20–50,000 square metres in area. They are in effect superstore feeders, the scale of their operations a mystery even to the people who pass by them every day.

Most imagine that they are warehouses, cheap and artless. In reality they are far more active, day and night. 'Big Sheds' combine perfect formal simplicity with a wonderful sophistication. At one level they are simple because they are 100 per cent recyclable. Because of the way they are put together their sandwich aluminium wall and roof panels can be torn off and melted down, and their steel structural frames can be cut up with oxy-acetylene torches and sold for scrap. Their laser-flat concrete floors can be broken up and sold for hard core. At another level they are sophisticated because, when in operation, their interiors burst with new technology. The cost of the computer-controlled mechanical handling equipment they contain can often exceed their construction cost. 'Big Sheds' are smart buildings, run by computerized building management systems and a small but heavily mechanized work force. Not only can they be operated by remote control from headquarters hundreds of miles away, but some of them have more sinister public functions too. The glistening aluminium walls of one distribution centre at Portbury enclose five acres of concentric cold stores surrounding one another like Russian dolls. At their heart is a deep-freeze chamber kept at minus 25 degrees Celsius. In the event of an air crash or similar disaster it would be requisitioned as a mortuary.

In a way this paradox of household names, frozen groceries and corpses epitomizes the futuristic aspect of Portbury. The same is true of the view that greets a driver cresting the rise that launches the western carriageway of the M5 down to the Avon Bridge. In sunlight it is a seascape whose glistening waves are not made of water but of cars: thousands of imported, unregistered Protons, Mitsubishis and Volvos unloaded from transporter ships at the docks and dense-packed into chainlink-fenced compounds waiting to be sold.

Portbury not only has some of the largest 'Big Shed' buildings in the country, it has three of the most unusual. These are

An aerial view of the 60,000-square-metre Lafarge Plasterboard factory at Portbury, a huge advanced-technology production facility that takes in raw gypsum by conveyor from bulk carriers in the docks, and dispatches 50 million square metres of new plasterboard every year.

pitched-roof 'cathedrals', immense and brilliant white triangular structures that are robot buildings of another kind. Two of them are brand new coal-importing and storage buildings. The third is one of the largest and most modern plasterboard factories in Europe. Because of their whiteness, their steep roofs and their prominent overhead conveyors, these three stand out from Portbury's sea of rectangular sheds like icebergs. They are cathedral-shaped because the 38-degree slope of their roofs follows the 'natural angle of repose' of coal and gypsum.

The first of these three distinctive buildings to be completed, and the largest, is a plasterboard factory that was originally built in 1989 and subsequently enlarged from 33,000 square metres to over 50,000 – the size of six World Cup stadiums. At the time of writing it is capable of producing 50 million square metres of plasterboard a year. Its soaring overhead conveyor can transport 1,500 tonnes of gypsum an hour a quarter of a mile from a docked self-unloading bulk carrier to the cathedral-shaped storage building. From there it is moved to the natural gas-powered plasterboard production facility, an even larger building that is kept at below atmospheric pressure so that it emits no dust, only an innocuous white plume of water vapour, given off by its drying machinery.

Two computer-generated images of the projected waste disposal facility at Bielefeld, Germany, designed by IPL Fabric Structures in 1994. The 120,000-square-metre air-supported membrane was intended to crawl across the landscape over a period of 30 years, shedding membrane panels behind it and refixing them in front. 85 per cent of the membrane panels were expected to be reusable.

The plasterboard factory cost £60 million to build, most of it spent on computer-controlled machinery. Two London firms of architects were involved in its design, Fitzroy Robinson and Partners and Stafford Moor and Farrington. The former firm has built many prestige office buildings in the City of London, including the St Martin's le Grand 'stealth building' described in Chapter 3. The latter firm is hardly known at all outside industrial circles. Such anonymity is part of the culture of 'Big Shed' architecture, with its miracles of functional design, carefully fitted around mechanical processes, vast, computerized, yet ignored. Seen from the air, the plasterboard factory at Portbury speaks for all of them. Like a diagram of the national economy, it reaches out its long conveyor to import raw materials at one end while, at the other, it feeds the adjoining motorway network with a stream of articulated trucks laden with finished products.

Anonymous, automated giants such as these give us an authentic *frisson* of the twenty-first century in ways that traditional big-name architecture never can, and in the future they are destined to give us more. For if today's 'Big Sheds' are already creating a huge new scale of landscape, then the flexible, air-supported structures that will succeed them are poised to go much further. They already resemble landscape itself rather than any conventional building. In Germany there are projects for huge, hermetically sealed landfill enclosures that literally are moving landscape. This new departure was first developed by the German fabric structure company Ingenieur Plannung Leichtbau – Light Structures Design and Engineering, or IPL – with its design for a 250 x 650-metre low-level 'roof 'covering a toxic waste site near the city of Bielefeld. An enormous envelope composed of hundreds of PVC polyester fabric panels criss-crossed by steel beams supported by air pressure, this £90 million enclosure was intended to crawl over the landscape for a period of 30 years, hermetically sealing toxic waste into lagoons from which no leakage into the surrounding soil was possible. The apparent movement of the envelope was to be achieved by continually dismantling and rebuilding its perimeter, while the sealing-off of fumes was to be maintained by a system of air locks, some big enough to drive trucks through. The performance of the whole membrane was to have been monitored by stress gauges and gas detectors 24 hours a day. It would thus have become not only the largest air-supported structure in the world, but a kind of architectural organism without precedent.

One hundred and fifty years before the first 'Big Shed' was built at Portbury, at a time when the idea of 'moving landscape' did not exist, knowledge was considered to be a matter of the printed word. Storing knowledge was therefore a matter of space to store books, and to this end a great circular reading room was erected for the library of the British Museum. A *tour de force* of Victorian engineering, the roof of this vast chamber, larger than the dome of St Peter's in Rome, rapidly came to enclose the greatest concentration of knowledge in the world. But that was a long time ago. One hundred and fifty years later it is apparent to all of us that the shape of knowledge has changed. In the McLuhan age, collections of books have lost their privileged status. Modern information systems have revealed them for what they are, fragile, limited-capacity pre-industrial cassettes of knowledge. Even the rarest and most valuable old books are no more than compressed rags, sewn together with cotton thread. Their covers are made from the skins of animals, their titles crudely embossed by hand. Even their type was set, letter by letter, in wooden frames. More and more, books are becoming curiosities from a bygone age.

Today we access knowledge by different means. We absorb it from moving pictures, live and recorded sound, signals bounced off satellites, documents duplicated, faxed, e-mailed or displayed on TV screens, from the worldwide web and the Internet. At the end of the twentieth century books have become little more than the 'cassettes' of an old-fashioned information system, containers of a knowledge that must be scanned and digitized in order to be available. Other systems work better. Even as our knowledge sources proliferate we miniaturize their output, recording it invisibly on magnetic tapes, microchips, CDs, hard and floppy disks, and crystals of enormous capacity.

It was in 1962, on the eve of this technological revolution and just over a century after the Reading Room was built, that the project for the construction of a new British Library was begun. The old library was by then thought to be inadequate, not because the farsighted administrators of the day

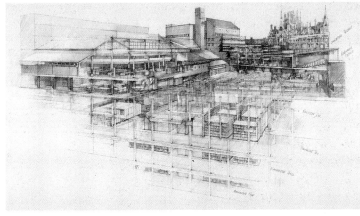

An artist's impression of the £600 million British Library building in London's Euston Road (architect: Colin St John Wilson). The architectural relationship to St Pancras Chambers is clear and exemplifies the power of the art-historical principle of the pre-eminence of the old.

A cutaway drawing of the British Library that offers an indication of the enormous complexity and cost incurred by the decision to locate the book stacks underground, and in an area laced with existing railway tunnels.

had anticipated the obsolescence of the book, but because it lacked sufficient storage space and the millions of books it already owned were disintegrating as a consequence of wear and tear and poor storage conditions. Build the right library building, it was thought, and devise a better book handling and storage system, and all these problems would dissappear for another hundred years.

Thirty-five years later this has not happened. Ever since the project to build what is now called the British Library began, the world of knowledge has been living through a volcanic eruption of new technology whose effect has been, if not to render the book entirely obsolete, at least to make its place in the future doubtful. Certainly from fifteenth-century Gutenberg to twentieth-century Marshall McLuhan the overwhelming bulk of the world's knowledge has been contained in books. But no such certainty exists now. We have discovered that, just as a refrigerator is no more than access to a volume of cold air, so is a library no more than a place where there is access to information: information that may be stored remotely, in books thousands of miles away, on silicon chips, compact discs or rolls of microfilm.

This of course is a deculturalized 'Terminal 2' view of the function of a library, according to which access to its store of information – kept perhaps in a 'Big Shed' out on the motor-way network – might as well be made by fax, modem or tele-phone from the enquirer's home or place of work, as by a journey to a grand bombastic cultural edifice in the centre of a city. Few would dare to say that the British Library next to St Pancras Station – 'One of the great pillars of civilization', as its chief executive officer has modestly described it – could have simply been a 'Big Shed', but why not?

The 'Terminal 1' library on the Euston Road that was finally opened in the autumn of 1997 had undergone a process of design, redesign and agonizingly slow construc-tion and fitting out for as long as most people could remem-ber. It had been allocated four different sites, been made the responsibility of five successive government departments, had five chairmen, three chief executives and two client

The British Library's own 'Big Shed' complex, the 60-acre book depository at Boston Spa in Yorkshire, from where 90 per cent of the British Library's business is transacted.

bodies. All this had involved the expenditure of a line of credit exceeding £600 million. Vast amounts of money were thrown at it, only to be clawed back in savage cuts, and savage cuts in turn were succeeded by grudging gifts of more money. As political attitudes, national fortunes, library technology, information science, conservation and utopianism waxed and waned, so did the building mutate over 35 years from an architectural masterpiece into a treasure house of rare books, from a treasure house of books to a magnificent setting for great Modern works of art, and from a magnificent setting for great works of art into a world centre for information technology and distance learning. And all this took place largely in the mind! For not one of these grand identities was to be seen in action on the ground. True, there is now a building on the Euston Road called the British Library. True, it will house 12 million monographs, 280,000 manuscripts, 8 million stamps, 1 million maps, 1 million music scores, 32 million patent specifications and so on. But it has long since been admitted that it is not really capable of replacing its Bloomsbury predecessor. Already there has been trouble with its automated book handling system, with its shelving, and with delays and arguments with the publishing industry over copyright. Already we know that, far from providing extra space, it could have been full to capacity the day of its long-delayed opening. Most important of all, we know that without its vast but undistinguished 'Big Shed' satellite at Boston Spa, in Yorkshire – the 60-acre book depository that handles 93 per cent of all requests to the library by means of a mass photocopying and electronic data transmission service supplying 22,000 customers a day – the British Library would not be a British Library at all.

At the opposite extreme to the lavish, generation-long, 'Terminal 1' saga of the British Library is the Cadbury's Easter egg depository at Minworth, near Birmingham. This is very definitely a 'Terminal 2' structure. Designed and built in only 18 months at a total cost of £24 million – half of which was spent on the computer-controlled mechanical handling equipment inside it – the Minford depository is a very large, pressurized, condensation-free chilled store that was opened in September 1993. At 40,000 square metres, its floor area is less than half that of the British Library. Yet, although the

The Cadbury Easter Egg store and distribution centre at Minworth, Birmingham. It cost £24 million instead of £600 million and took 18 months instead of 35 years to build.

comparison might seem outlandish, the job it does is not very different to that carried out by Boston Spa, where the real business of the British Library is transacted. Under carefully controlled conditions Minworth receives, stores and dispatches huge numbers of Easter eggs, vulnerable items that require handling at least as carefully as books. Easter eggs have only one selling season a year yet, unlike the British Library, with its elaborate art-historical 'Terminal 1' superstructure and its impossible-to-waterproof maze of underground book stacks, Minworth is a bland, even crass above-ground building all on one floor. The arrival and departure of the eggs that are its 'books' is completely mechanized. They pass through twenty conventional loading bays, or one of two Hydra-Roll automatic unloaders that can empty a full-sized articulated lorry of all its pallets in just two minutes. Six robot electric trains following buried guide cables carry the eggs to and from an array of manned mobile cranes that serve the miles of high-density racking that occupy the bulk of the building. Stored in that racking, up to 30 million chocolate eggs can be kept at controlled humidity and a constant temperature of 6 degrees Celsius, winter and summer alike – a climatic toler-ance better than that achieved in the Reading Room at the British Museum and comparable to that of the new British Library. So efficient is Minworth's operation that it has replaced thirteen smaller warehouses and requires a staff of only sixteen, working shifts, to keep it in operation 24 hours a day.

The difference between these two buildings might seem at first too obvious and trivial to make a serious point, but it is not. There are sound technical reasons for arguing that an above-ground 'Big Shed', automated in the manner of the Minworth depository, would have made a much better British Library than the one we have now, even if it had to be built on the same site in the Euston Road. A 'Big Shed' British Library would not only have been in service in *one twenty-third of the time* it took the present building to come on stream: if necessary it could have been built and rebuilt *twenty-four times* in response to rapidly evolving information technologies, all for less money than was spent on the sculpture-bedecked British Library.

In the information age there is no market for a computer system delivered three years too late, an airliner with insufficient range to reach its destination, or a non-industry standard recording device. When a building is commissioned into a knowledge environment, yet fails as spectacularly as the British Library has failed – by being so late that its anticipated functions have been overtaken by events – it is clearly obsolete. To counter that such a building is a 'Terminal 1' architectural masterpiece and a treasure house of priceless historical artefacts is to miss the point. As Charles Darwin insisted, it is futile to take pity on an ill-adapted species just because its environment is hostile. All species must conform to the demands of their environment or die.

'Big Shed' architecture is a post-Modern phenomenon. It began in earnest in the early 1970s when all over Europe, in a great dorsal belt running from the English Midlands to the Mezzo Giorno, the new distribution landscape of the European Community first began to come together. In place of traditional town and city locations, giant mechanized distribution-centre floorspace began to be constructed at breakneck speed at thousands of exits and intersections on nearly 50,000 kilometres of autoroute. During the 1980s a million out-of-town commercial and retail centres sprang up to join them, with no reference to the fate of the ancient town and city centre sites left behind. In England alone 100 out-of-town shopping centres were projected between 1985 and 1989, nearly half of them planned to include more than 100,000 square metres of covered floorspace, and no fewer than nine

The concept of a plug-in building, used as an electricity advertisement in the 1970s, is now a key principle for all non-art-historical architecture.

of them projected for sites on the M25 London orbital motorway then nearing completion.

All the 'Big Shed' buildings completed during this period are part of the unsentimental, computer-generated face of Terminal Architecture. Planners and architects played only a minor role in the production and operation of these vast 'zero-defect' enclosures, devoid as they were of any art-historical identity. These blank-walled buildings were visible manifestations of the abstract, invisible, digital network that now links all the EC countries and their neighbours in a seamless web of production, distribution and consumption. They are part of a network of terminals linked by schedules and journeys that work a 24-hour day through container ports, airports and railway stations, automated freezer stores, sealed warehouses, vast truck parks and transient dormitories of mobile homes.

At present this 'digital urbanism' (its 'towns' are often only designated by numbered autoroute exits) is culturally ignored. Yet in economic terms it is already of far greater importance than anything built inside the old towns and cities it has bypassed. Unlike heritage architecture, which has the vast literature of tourism to support it, this is, in the terminology of the immigration officer, 'undocumented' construction. There is no cultural literature to document it. No novelist or film maker explores beneath its surface. Who in the arts knows anything about the culture of truck drivers who sleep in tiny capsules above the cabs of their trucks, their positions plotted and checked by satellite? Which gallery curator comprehends the space occupied by those who sit, day after day, in front of video monitors? Who chronicles the doings of fork-lift truck drivers, checkout persons, air traffic controllers, control room operators, computer trouble-shooters, ambulance men, mechanics, linemen, canteen operatives, cash card loaders, vending machine loaders, photo-copier repairers, stacking crane drivers or security guards? These are the prototype non-communal persons of the future, denizens of the 'Big Shed' universe, linked to one another only by the global heartbeat of FM radio and satellite TV.

The Australian architect and industrial designer Michael Trudgeon has seen very clearly what Terminal Architecture means in terms of a revolution in architectural design. In a 1993 magazine interview he was quoted as follows on the enormous disparity between the number of design hours

A computer-generated image of part of Michael Trudgeon's 'Hyper House'. The glass walls are supported by aluminium mullions with integrated drainage channels. With the compound curvature facility of a car body, the hypocycloid corners of the floor metamorphose into an elliptical roof plan. The single supporting column in the centre contains thermal batteries.

invested in the development of a complex industrial product like a new motor car, and the number of design hours invested in new buildings:

A totally new Japanese car requires 1.7 million hours of research and development time from a blank sheet of paper to the first customer delivery. With an average production run of one million cars, the design cost amortized across the production run comes in at only $425 per car, but each car has the benefit of 1.7 million hours of design thought. By comparison a new office building, costing $50 million with design consultancy fees running at 5 per cent of cost, has the benefit of only 10,000 hours of design thought. The worst case of all is a three-bedroom architect-designed family home, with fees running at 11 per cent of cost. This will have only 1,750 hours of design thought. Under these conditions it is ridiculous to talk about 'smart buildings'.[2]

Trudgeon's own response to the want of design time for conventional architecture has been to issue a specification for a prototype industrial dwelling, approaching the problem as he believed a car manufacturer might approach it. First conceived in 1992 and still under development, his 'Hyper House' project treated the dwelling as a multifunctional living space enclosed by an intelligent skin, in the form of a chemically-treated glass membrane capable of generating variable privacy, views out, and high or low insulation values. In his own words this skin 'acts as a chameleon-like canvas wrapped around a TV screen', generating sampled images, textures, graphics and text.

The living space enclosed within this skin is to be serviced using systems manufactured to car industry product standards, leased and serviceable, like computers, video recorders or aircraft sub-assemblies – for example a roll-in, roll-out bathroom modelled on passenger aircraft toilet modules, equipped with a mechanical vapour recompression water recycling unit, and a single arterial service loop from which sewage, clean water, optical, data and telephone links can be accessed at any point required. The external envelope of the dwelling itself will be cleaned and maintained by a crawling 'service limpet' as though it were the hull of a supertanker.

Described in this way it is clear that Trudgeon's 'Hyper

House' is an appropriate subject for 500,000 hours of design work. He wants it to respond to climatic changes and the demands of its occupants through an array of sensors connected to a network of small control computers. It will be able to store energy with its own structure acting as a thermal battery. He likens it to a kind of mechanical mammal, sharing the same ability to conserve internal 'body heat' by controlling the permeability of its skin. Structurally the dwelling will be a kit of parts snap-locked together from an ever-expanding array of components adding up to an infinitely upgradable product. The house will thus become a static customized car, with a different equipment package available for every owner. In this it leaves the realm of architectural design and joins the realm of industrial design instead, becoming a model for Terminal Architecture in the process.

As a mechanism to speed the arrival of advanced industrial shelter products like the 'Hyper House', conventional architectural design has little to offer. Too little design time and minimal performance targets make it a methodology that actually stands in the way of industrialization, holding much of the construction industry back even from the standards of sophistication associated with the production and assembly of 'Big Sheds'. In Trudgeon's view architecture has become 'an anti-technological virus', an antibody that prevents the machine culture of design from spreading out from high-tech manufacturing industry to engulf the construction process. Kill off that virus and the machine culture of design will soon determine the shape of the terminal world, for in all fields save architecture it has already displaced ideology as the connecting link between human needs and available resources.

One terminal building type that has in the past benefited from relatively high levels of design input is the petrol station. Like 'Big Sheds' all modern petrol stations are deceptively simple in appearance but are in fact sophisticated three-dimensional structures. For years they have evaded the anti-technological virus of architecture by drawing on the design resources of the motor industry and the huge materials base of plastics, derived from petroleum, their parent fuel.

Like icebergs, most of the bulk of a petrol station is invisible, typically taking the form of 60,000 litres of petrol and oil in tanks under the ground. Above these tanks is a paved

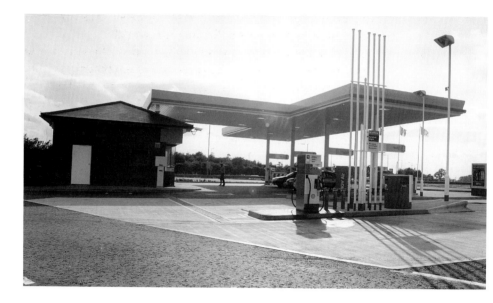

forecourt dotted with pumps, canopies, car washes, mono-liths (the totem poles with the petrol prices on them) and small shops. It is this upstairs-downstairs configuration that makes it relatively easy to update the topsides of a petrol station with a new look, like a car body on a chassis. The difference is that not only most of the forecourt pieces in a petrol station but the underground tank linings and pipe-work too are made entirely of plastic, which in turn is made from petroleum, which is the product the oil company sells. In this sense the petrol station is a perfect example of Saint Exupéry's observation that 'Every machine will lose its iden-tity in function'.[3] Structure and merchandise both come from the same source. It is as though a home with gas central heat-ing were actually made out of gas. A petrol station is a piece of chemical magic made of space, energy and information, and nothing else.

This strange chemistry is the reason why, to understand petrol station design, it is necessary to think about it in a dif-ferent way to more conventional buildings. Its shape and purpose have entered popular mythology as a different kind of symbol altogether, one of enthusiasm for the rootless mobility of the automobile age. Over the years successive artists and film makers have captured the strange mixture of emotions generated by the enigmatic architecture and sociology of the filling station as a structure alien to its immediate

Rear view of the Shell RVI petrol station at Littleover, Derby. Apart from the brick and slate shop called for by planners, the rest is minimalist sophistication, with its complexity sublimated in its function.

surroundings, but indissolubly tied to the endless ribbon of road that links all places in the modern world.

Petrol stations are not architecture incidentally attached to a massive processing and distribution system that starts from an oil platform in the North Sea. They are the product of their own product. The typical petrol station is not a 'Terminal 1' art-historical object, but a 'Terminal 2' product of industrial design, something more akin to an enormous vending machine, one of the largest pieces of non-mobile, freestanding product design in the world. It is because petrol station designers have been free of art-historical criticism that even their most mundane product is so refined, so attenuated, so minimalist and so instantly recognizable. Like 'Big Sheds', all the operations of petrol stations, from routine maintenance to tanker visits, can be controlled by computer from operations centres hundreds of miles away. Petrol prices, the only prices denominated in fractions of a penny, can be simultaneously changed at pump, monolith and cash register in the same way. Nor is this the ultimate level of automation. Unmanned petrol stations, where payment is made using a credit card, are increasingly common, while completely robotized forecourts where the driver need not even leave his or her car are already in use experimentally.

Because of their complex and evolving design background, and the global reach of all the major oil companies, the redesign and harmonization of an international chain of petrol stations is a momentous event. The recently introduced Shell RVI design is a good example. The first step was taken in November 1989 when a group of senior executives of the Shell Group of Companies met at the Awana Golf and Country Club, near Kuala Lumpur in Malaysia. The details of their conference are secret, but what came out of it was one of the most ambitious industrial design projects of the twentieth century. Shell had decided to redesign their petrol stations all over the world at a cost outside observers estimated would be at least £4 billion. Because Shell was at that time the world's largest retailer, with three times as many outlets as the McDonalds hamburger chain, the world to them meant 40,000 petrol stations in 100 countries.

Shell's chosen design, called 'RVI', standing for Retail Visual Identity, like Michael Trudgeon's new Japanese car, was allocated thousands of hours of design time, including market

Large temperature-controlled agricultural storage buildings on a site in Essex.

Second World War aircraft hangars being demolished at Magna Park in Warwickshire in 1989. Magna Park, a former airbase known as RAF Bitteswell, lies at the centre of the M1/M6/M69 triangle and was for a time the largest distribution complex in Europe.

research in twelve countries and the design work of Addison Associates, later part of Wolf Olins. All the components of an RVI filling station, from its subtly curved, light-reflecting acrylic fascia to its flat – not corrugated – canopy underside, are fitted together as neatly as the body panels of a car. Here Shell's global reach helps, for economies of scale have enabled RVI to be based on precision 'production line' plastics, like satin acrylic, instead of locally hand laid-up glass fibre. Nor does the terminality of the petrol station stop with its construction. By the mid-1990s full RVI conversions in the United Kingdom were taking place at the rate of seven per week.

Characteristically, just as the architectural profession has only a tangential relationship with 'Big Sheds',[4] so does it tend to ignore the design quality of petrol stations. When in 1990 *Country Life* magazine published a diatribe against modern petrol stations accompanied by a number of architect designs for Palladian, Gothic, rustic and even camouflaged alternatives, some feared a concerted backlash against the RVI programme, but it did not materialize. Commenting in 1994, a Shell representative said, 'We don't have difficulties with planning officers, but the architects on the planning preview committees are a different matter. They look at our applications and recommend refusal to the planners. But even they don't want petrol stations that look like Georgian houses. They want real Georgian houses. They don't want petrol stations at all, even though they all drive cars.'[5]

The twentieth century has seen so many technical innovations emanating from the electronics industry that the day-to-day life of a citizen of 100 years ago seems almost unimaginably primitive. Even dwelling houses, which have hardly changed at all in appearance, show innumerable changes beneath the skin. Yet there is one area where all buildings seem reluctant to adopt a truly terminal stance and step into the twenty-first century, and that is in the matter of optical illusion. Despite the advent of virtual reality, permanent, unvarying external appearance and negligible internal exploitation of the possibilities of virtual space have been an architectural constant, from the beginning of our century to its end.

From the pioneering Modern architecture of the 1927 Weissenhof exhibition in Stuttgart to the Milton Keynes 'Futureworld' competition of 1994, all architectural 'homes of the future' have been futuristic only to the extent that they have used non-traditional materials and displayed different arrangements of walls, windows and floor plans. Roof gardens, freeform and open plans, unorthodox sections, air-conditioning, double glazing, domestic robots: none of these has ever changed the dwelling's commitment to real time and unchanging space. In this sense it is true to say that the perceived spatial limitations of all buildings, except cinemas, drive-in cinemas, exhibition pavilions and multiscreen, 3-D or IMAX theatres, remain limited by the acceptance of structural space definition in an era when structure need only serve as a framework for the illusory reality of virtual worlds.

Apart from the commercial building types identified above, which are deliberately designed to exploit spatial distortion for the purpose of entertainment, there is very little evidence of any deliberate architectural attempt to explore the impact of spatially distorting electronic imagery. In fact any such investigation is discouraged whenever architects hold, as many do, that virtual reality spells the end of all architecture.[6] The best-known architect to have penetrated beyond this point is the Japanese Toyo Ito, who is intensely interested in the impact of electronic media upon architecture and has been quoted in Chapter 8 on the subject.

In his 1989 Tower of the Winds, a temporary urban structure erected in Tokyo and since removed, Ito produced a cylindrical tower whose apparent configuration continuously

A mobile home with satellite antenna in Arizona, 1989. Prototype for the kind of 21st-century terminal dwelling submerged into the landscape that is represented in the illustration on page 167.

The initial concept of the VAP 'Futureworld' competition entry: a pod, like a small space capsule, with an internal video environment like the artificial horizon of an aircraft.

changed through the agency of computer-controlled lighting effects driven by changes in wind force and direction. Since then he has tried different approaches. In 1992 he based the design of his competition entry for the University of Paris Jussieu Library on the much magnified circuitry of a microchip. Most recently he won a competition to design a mediatheque for the city of Sendai, north of Tokyo, with a glass-clad project whose stacked floors emulated the shape of floppy disks, which he called 'media plates'. These plates were penetrated and supported by hollow geodesic columns providing communication between the different levels. The resultant building, highly transparent and structurally attenuated, Ito describes as 'a new image of space'.

At the time of writing Toyo Ito's view of the correct line to be followed by architecture in the information age follows this last precedent. He is quoted as having said, 'I do not think that architecture should be replaced with video images, or that temporary buildings should be used. We should rather build fictional and ephemeral architecture as a permanent entity.' To this end his present tendency is to 'dematerialize' his buildings by reducing the mass of their construction to a minimum. Perhaps with less fanatical attention to detail, but also at much lower cost, this has been the direction taken by the designers of 'Big Sheds' and petrol stations for many years. However, Ito clearly sees further ahead for he has also stated that 'the invasion of new media into architecture will not permit the survival of fixed, static form'.[7]

The next move beyond this position adopted by Ito requires, first of all, a reversal of his veto on video images for the internal definition of space, ideally coupled with a non-structural means of changing the apparent identity of an elementary 'Big Shed' envelope. To the author's knowledge little or nothing has been done along these lines. However, in their unplaced entry for the *Futureworld* 1993 'Home of the Future' competition, the Virtual Architecture Partnership (VAP) did design a variable-identity dwelling, capable of transforming its external appearance through the alignment of different images on three-sided rotating louvres, and transforming its apparent interior volume by means of video walls. In this way the identity of the outside of the house and the perceived shape of the interior were both freed from static formal constraints and opened up to the realm of interactive, immersive experience. Despite the rudimentary means employed, this project was truly terminal in so far as control over its inner and outer appearance depended entirely on a continuous flow of continuous electric current. In this project the concept of the house reached out to join the virtual reality of arcade video games and the IMAX cinema, demonstrating that exciting sensory experiences involving loss of orientation, time distortion and spatial anomaly need not be confined to screens or helmets, but could actually be lived as a domestic environment. Two subsequent VAP projects, one for a virtual reality 'House of the Future' to be part of a theme park in Barcelona, and the second proposed as an engineering study for a black-box office building with an artificial internal environment, were to have employed 3-D stereo projection in addition to video walls.[8]

South elevation 1:20

For different reasons the Terminal Architecture of the 'Big Shed', the petrol station and the virtual reality building are all out of the mainstream of architecture. All of them are conceived in a different way and according to 'Terminal 2' scales of value. Yet because of this they illuminate the forgotten essence of architectural design, which is not art-historical nor cultural but functional, in the end simply a life-servicing technology expressed as covered floorspace. Culturally excommunicated architecture of this kind can be beautiful, just as a ship, a truck or an aircraft can be beautiful, but once it is no longer required to adhere to a permanent form or a permanent space, there is no need for it to be individually 'creative' or 'intellectual'. Nor is it required of designers that they should drive themselves mad, like painters putting up a fight against photography, by trying to design 'abstract buildings', like paintings by Picasso, Braque, or Nonja, the artist chimpanzee...

The issue of originality is an interesting issue in this context, and indeed an old one, having been the turning point of legal actions brought by and against artists in the nineteenth century.[9] A more recent case, which has already been mentioned, is exemplary because it involved undeclared originality. This came to light in 1935 when the celebrated violinist Fritz Kreisler admitted to a journalist that for 30 years he had been inserting pieces of his own composition into recitals of

An elevation of the VAP 'Futureworld' competition entry, showing the variable external identity achieved by means of commercial rotating advertising signs.

A distribution centre at Magna Park seen from a distance. 'Another kind of building altogether, a type so large, so numerous and so anonymous that it does not appear on ordnance survey maps, is not kept up to date by aerial photographic surveys, and is in all other respects almost completely ignored.'

the works of seventeenth- and eighteenth-century composers. Kreisler came under savage attack but he was unrepentant. If his listeners could not distinguish between the pieces he played and genuine baroque music, he argued, why should it matter whether they were forged or not?

The Kreisler episode has its analogues in architecture today. Architecture, like music, is inextricably bound up with the exalted myth of individual creativity that Kreisler exposed. Why this should be is not clear. All architects know, notwithstanding recent legislation permitting the registration of their designs, that their buildings are not really intellectual property in the same way as paintings, patents or musical compositions. Building a building is more like winning an election than writing a book. It is a process involving a cast of hundreds, if not thousands, of whom the architect is the only actor who may be trying to produce something original. The more architecture becomes a matter of combining finished assemblies, the more design time will be applied to it and the more consultants will become involved. Logically, therefore, the more certain it will become that architects will have to share, or move away from meretricious claims of creativity and 'meaning'. Sooner or later they will follow the advice of the perspicacious Adolf Loos, who wrote a century ago, 'We have enough original geniuses, why don't we repeat ourselves endlessly instead?'[10]

Why not indeed? Because of the loss of 'individual creativity' in the built environment? Lasers, electronics, holography and video graphics are already beginning to relieve architects of this burden. What will remain for Terminal Architecture will be the sort of pure 'zero-defect' design that produces those modern paradigms of technological perfection: the motor car, the airliner, the racing yacht and the precision metal cladding system. Why this should not be a source of pride is a psychological matter connected with the self-image of the architectural profession. Few celebrity architects today are prepared to jettison their art-historical pretensions and admit that the design of buildings in the future is destined to be a process founded on the pursuit of technology transfers, every one of them passed beneath the Occam's razor of Richard Buckminster Fuller's first law of technological evolution, which says that the only valid measure of success is the capacity to achieve better results with fewer resources. To do this would be to admit that architectural design is no longer 'creative' in the old 'Terminal 1' sense, but 'mechanical', in the 'Terminal 2' sense that it depends upon a process of multi-sourced element combination that can better be systematized than created anew for every job.

Established on a proper financial footing, a research organization devoted to the task of creating the first architects' technology transfer data base could open up the key process of finished element combination so that it brings together the anonymity of the 'hot site', the efficiency of the 'Big Shed', the ephemeralization of the petrol station, and the limitless horizons of virtual reality, and exposes all of them to the methodology of automated industrial production. Such a project may sound more difficult than opening yet another architecture centre, or continuing to invent new tunes for old composers, but it is an enterprise that is admirably suited to the skills of the practitioners of Terminal Architecture.

Ultra fast, dirt cheap and error-free, depopulated instead

of overpopulated, the architectural profession that survives into the twenty-first century has the opportunity to become a producer of instruments, not a creator of monuments. It need no longer be enslaved by ideas of value drawn from the 'treasure houses' and museums of antiquity. Instead it will be free to exploit the products of research and development in every developing field of technology, living like a parasite upon the body of all productive industry, from aerospace to biotechnology – a paperless profession that will travel light, relying on electronic brainwork instead of voodoo symbolism and the tribal taboo of the past.

References

2 FROM COLD WAR TO NEW REALITY

1 'The big full-service architecture, engineering and construction firm is going to become as much of a dinosaur as the Soviet aerospace industry. With bigger projects and fewer repeat clients, only a handful of globalized consortiums will be able to afford to carry all that talent on a loss ratio of 20 or 50 jobs to one.' *World Architecture*, No. 50, October 1966, p. 35.

2 A construction industry reorganized along corporate lines would undoubtedly dismantle the independent professions and relocate their active members as employees. At the same time it would reach market accommodations in all sectors and differentiate models logically, as does the motor industry.

3 An example of this feedback error came to light in 1997 in connection with the theory of global warming. So many scientists had by then publicly endorsed the view that the survival of our planet depends upon drastically cutting the output of man-made 'greenhouse gases' that governments had begun justifying taxes on fuel on this basis. The only problem with this theory was that actual terrestrial temperature measurements over the last 100 years only showed an increase of between 0.3 and 0.6 of a degree Celsius instead of the much larger increase that computer modelling of 'global warming' had predicted. Worse still, even this small increase was thrown into doubt by measurements of the temperature of the lower atmosphere taken by scientific satellites looking down from space. These monitors showed no increase at all over a period of twenty years, and in some cases recorded an actual decline. Despite the long history of human error in such situations, so many scientific reputations and so much national and international policy now hinges on the myth of global warming, that the majority of scientists are in favour of disregarding the contradictory satellite evidence altogether. 'Is the Earth really getting hotter?' *The Times*, 13 October 1997.

4 Despite his extraordinary importance in the history of radio, television and electronics there is very little comprehensive literature about Guglielmo Marconi, who posthumously fell from favour in England because of his associations with Italian Fascism between 1922 and 1937. The nearest to a comprehensive history is to be found in William Baker, *A History of the Marconi Company* (London, 1970).

5 A discussion of the posthumous life of John Wayne appeared in *The Sunday Times* of 18 August 1996 under the title 'Wayne rides back as all-American hero in land of modem cowboy'. Diana, Princess of Wales, can no doubt look forward to a similar synthetic immortality.

6 Simon Jenkins, 'Sue us, Your Majesties', *The Times*, 12 October, 1996.

7 'Lookalikes who earn money at the double', *The Sunday Times*, 22 September 1996.

8 Elton John's adapted version of his song 'Candle in the Wind', played and sung at the funeral of Diana, Princess of Wales, took only one month to sell 32 million copies and become the bestselling single of all time, a record previously held by Bing Crosby's 'White Christmas' with cumulative sales over 55 years. Total earnings for charity alone of the Elton John single were predicted to exceed £100 million.

9   These details of the sponsorship arrangements for the BT Global Challenge round-the-world yacht race were supplied by Malcolm McKeag to *The European*, 19–25 September 1996.

3   LONDON'S UNLUCKY TOWERS

1   The bulk of the information about Ronan Point in this chapter is taken from the news pages of *The Architects' Journal* in the relevant years, and from Miles Glendinning and Stefan Muthesius, *Tower Block*, (London 1994).

2   For example 'The Godsend that started cracking up', *The London Evening Standard*, 3 August 1984, in which the retired chief architect of Newham council reveals to a reporter that, in the 1960s, 'The choice of a prefabricated system of building was virtually forced on us. We had to find a way of meeting the housing targets.' Also, 'Such a charming carbuncle builder', *The Sunday Times*, 13 December 1987, in which Valerie Grove meets the retired architect of the twelve-storey Eleanor Rathbone House ('Dr Marmorek is not a wicked man. . .').

3   This idea lurks behind all Prince Charles's attacks on expertise. In his celebrated speech to architects at Hampton Court on 30 May 1984 he said, 'Architects and planners do not have a monopoly of knowing best about taste, style and planning. Ordinary people should not be made to feel guilty or ignorant if their natural preference is for more traditional designs.' Four years later, on 15 September 1988, he rounded on TV and film executives at the opening of the Museum of the Moving Image with the same idea: 'It is palpable nonsense to say that violence on TV has no effect on people's behaviour. The people who say this are so-called experts who attempt to confuse ordinary people so they feel they do not know what they are talking about.'

4   This estimate is derived from the projected loss over 21 years of £12.9 million calculated by Oliver Marriott in *The Property Boom*, (London, 1967). Understandably Marriott's figure underestimates the effects of inflation, particularly in the 1970s. *The Property Boom* is an invaluable source for information about Centre Point.

5   All but forgotten, this period featured the construction of London Wall, lined with towers, the high-rise Barbican estate, the National Westminster drive-in bank in Lombard Street, underground car parks and many other Modern structures. Subjected to the derision of a later period, most of these are displayed in the pamphlet 'From Splendour to Banality: The Rebuilding of the City of London', published in 1983 by Save Britain's Heritage.

6   The double-decker lifts were a mixed blessing. Stopping at two floors instead of one, and with one deck dedicated to high-ranking executives with their own operator, the occupants of the second deck were sometimes swept away on executive missions. *The Sunday Times Magazine*, 16 March 1980.

7   Both the big City bombs seriously damaged the economy of the City. Landmark financial services buildings were blitzed and took years to repair. So on-target were the two monster IRA bombs that the second actually disrupted a meeting of the council of the European Bank of Reconstruction and Development (EBRD). Within a week of this event direct warnings of departure from London by several foreign banks were received by the City Corporation and the British government. Unless the City could be made safe, said the overseas banks, they would relocate to Brussels, Paris or Frankfurt.

8   This sheer tonnage of financial services building seems ironic when its sequel is brought to mind. In the boom years of the 1980s, about 190,000

extra jobs were created in financial and business services in London. According to St Quintin's research report, 'The City of London to the Year 2000 and Beyond', the global stock market crash of 1987 led to the loss of 110,000 of these jobs, with the City the hardest-hit part of London, losing 50,000 jobs between 1990 and 1993. Professor Amin Rajan, director of the Centre for Research in Employment and Technology in Europe, is quoted as believing that 'All service organizations are now exposed to the same forces that started the terminal decline of many manufacturing industries after the recessions of 1974–5 and 1979–81.'

9 The best summary of the construction of Canary Wharf Tower is 'Canary Wharf: a landmark in construction', a supplement produced by *Building* magazine in October 1991.

10 Kvaerner and Foster & Partners stated their belief that the tower, in its original 95-storey, 385-metre form, could have been built in 48 months from the date of permission, only twelve months longer than the time taken to build the Canary Wharf Tower, despite the extra 145 metres in height, the difficult site access and the extra 40,000 square metres of floor area to be enclosed.

4 THE SKYSCRAPER GOES EAST

1 Louis Henry Sullivan's autobiography, *The Autobiography of an Idea* (New York, 1924), recounts the author's struggle to establish a functional steel-frame architecture in America. Sullivan laid claim to the axiom 'Form follows function', which he claimed to have evolved 'through long contemplation of living things'. He was firm in his conviction 'that no architectural dictum or tradition or superstition or habit should stand in the way of making an architecture that fitted its functions – a realistic architecture based on well-defined utilitarian needs'.

2 Despite this rapid eclipse the Chrysler Building has continued to exercise a powerful influence over later generations of architects. The Chinese architect C.Y. Lee has cited it as his inspiration for much of the formal richness of the Grand 50 and the T&C Tower.

3 An account of the career of C.Y. Lee and details of the Grand 50 and the T&C Tower and other Taiwanese high-rise buildings can be found in *World Architecture*, No. 54, March 1997.

4 The history of Japanese involvement with ultra-high towers and the concept of vertical urbanism traces back a generation. In 1966 Richard Buckminster Fuller designed a tripod structure 4,000 metres high – 200 metres higher than the summit of Mount Fuji – for the Yomiuri Corporation, which was to have featured a pressurized observation capsule 30 storeys tall providing a 360-degree view of all the Japanese islands. Apartment complexes built around each leg of the tripod would have been taller than the Eiffel Tower. Costed at US$1.5 billion in 1966, the project technically remains on hold to this day but has in effect been abandoned.

5 The prospects are already bright. In Shanghai at present the tallest structure is the China TV tower in Pudong, which reaches to 480 metres. This will soon be joined by the 94-storey, 460-metre Shanghai World Financial Centre, designed by the American architects Kohn Pedersen Fox; and the 88-storey, 418-metre combined office block and hotel Jin Mao building by SOM, also architects for the projected 66-storey Post and Telecommunications Tower in Xiamen. Construction of the World Financial Centre, which will be taller than the Kuala Lumpur 449-metre Petronas Towers, began in September 1997. A lower Shanghai contender is the projected 288-metre Wan Xiang International Plaza on Nanjing Road, by the German architects Ingenhoven Overdiek Kahlen und Partner.

6 According to the *World Architecture* 'Top 200' Survey for 1998. *World Architecture,* No. 62, December/January 1998.

7 The migration of capital and development expertise from Europe and North America to East Asia following the collapse of property markets in the early 1990s would repay detailed study. Certainly whole teams of professionals left London precipitately for the Far East following the failure of several property companies, notably the Canary Wharf developers Olympia & York in 1992. American architects too combed South East Asia, drafting schemes overnight for Asian entrepreneurs using the doors of hotel bathrooms as drawing boards.

8 As Tony FitzPatrick, director of Ove Arup & Partners, puts it bluntly: 'A building like the London Millennium Tower, with 2,000-square-metre floor plates, has an immediate 50 per cent operating cost advantage over any number of five-storey buildings with 500-square-metre floor plates. In fact five-storey buildings with 500-square-metre floor plates are an energy disaster.' 'The Arup Archipelago', *World Architecture,* No. 57, June 1997.

9 The Mansion House Square project was the brainchild of the developer Peter Palumbo (later Lord Palumbo). It involved the demolition of two buildings near the Mansion House in the City, permitting the creation of a public square adjoining Queen Victoria Street. Facing this square a 70-metre office tower designed by Mies van der Rohe was to have been built. Although it matured over twenty years this wholly beneficial scheme was refused planning permission by the Court of Common Council and was defeated on appeal by a consortium of conservationist organizations. The project was succeeded by the much smaller No.1 Poultry project for a low-rise building designed by Sir James Stirling.

5 OVER THE TOP WITH ART HISTORY

1 See the author's *Theory and Design in the Second Machine Age* for an earlier exploration of the mutiny analogy.

2 In which connection the life of the pioneer art critic Denis Diderot (1713–84) can be considered an early venture.

3 Quoted in William Gaunt, *The Aesthetic Adventure* (1945).

4 See the author's *Architecture versus Housing* (1971).

5 What other descriptor could do justice to the organization formed to deliver Modernism into the hands of art history in return for a promise that part of heritage largesse would in future be spent on the patching up of Modern ruins?

6 'Lubetkin Speaks', interview with Berthold Lubetkin, *Building Design,* 12 March 1982, p. 8.

7 Roger Scruton, 'Art History and Aesthetic Judgement', in *The Classical Vernacular,* 1994.

8 The first is from T. R. Willey, *The Early Renaissance* (1955), and the second from Gaunt (*ibid*).

9 The term 'saturated' is used here in the photographic sense. It refers to a technique for giving enhanced brilliance to colours by artificial means.

10 Sir Jocelyn Stevens, discourse given at the Bovis Construction and *Architects' Journal* Awards for Architecture dinner, 1996.

11 Nonetheless it is impossible to resist quoting *The Times* of 7 November 1996 on Eric Hebborn, who flooded the art market with more than a thousand fake Old Masters over a period of 30 years. Asked how Hebborn convinced buyers that his work was genuine, his partner Graham David Smith replied, 'He didn't need to. All he had to do was approach a dealer and say, "I've found this rather early drawing. What do you think?"'

12 For example, the discovery that a drawing of a bicycle that has been attributed to Leonardo da Vinci since its discovery in 1974, subsequently

'reconstructed' in wood and displayed as late as 1997 in a New York exhibition, is in fact a doodle made by a monk in the 1960s (*The Times*, 16 October 1997). Or the repeated assertions that the National Gallery's *Samson and Delilah* by Rubens, purchased at auction in 1980 for £2 million, is in fact a fake 'painted by apprentices' (*The Sunday Times*, 5 October 1997). Or the twin revelations that one of the three famous van Gogh Sunflower paintings is a copy, and that Sir Christopher Wren was responsible for the design of only four of the 50 London churches generally attributed to him (both in *The Sunday Times*, 26 October 1997).

13 For the extent of the use of fake art works in government buildings see 'Faker of the FO saves Old Masters for the nation' (*The Sunday Times*, 21 September 1997), in which a painter named Leo Stevenson cheerfully admits to having been commissioned to provide 'replica' art treasures for government buildings. Admiringly, the authors wrote, 'He recently painted *The Concert* by Vermeer and included, invisibly except by X-ray, the words "Elvis lives" under the lute.' In the same anarchic spirit, in 1995 Leon Carmen, a 47-year-old man from Sydney, won the prestigious Australian Doobie Award for the best first novel by a woman with *My Own Sweet Time*, submitted under the aboriginal name Wanda Koolmatrie. And in 1997 Elizabeth Durack, an 81-year-old white artist, admitted to pulling the same trick by inventing Eddie Burrup, an aboriginal farm worker who enjoyed fame for several years for his paintings, photographs and writings (*International Herald Tribune*, 14 March 1997). The child plagiarist story, in which the schoolgirl appears to be praised for her initiative, appeared as 'Plagiarist, 13, fools poetry judges' in *The Times*, 23 July 1997.

14 *The Times*, 2 October 1986. The quote is attributed to the stipendiary magistrate who disposed of the case brought against the Gormans by Thurrock District Council.

6 FROM MODERNISM TO POSTMODERNISM

1 For those dismayed by this speedy postponement of any consideration of the prospects for 'Green Architecture', I offer the conclusions of the Third European Conference on Solar Energy and Urban Planning held in Florence in 1993. At the planning stage the organizers had intended to issue a 'Florence Charter' for 'Green Architecture' to rival the Athens Charter promulgated by the International Congress of Modern Architecture in 1933. By the end of the conference this ambition had been watered down to a declaration that 'effective solar heating and cooling would be achieved within 100 years'. Compared to President Kennedy's Apollo Program, which vowed to put men on the moon in ten years, this seemed excessively cautious. But in fact it was almost recklessly ambitious. To achieve a truly 'Green Architecture', which means an architecture of buildings that can live off the 'income' energy of the sun (as opposed to its fossil fuel 'capital'), is no less intractable a project than to walk on the moon. 'Green Architecture' flirts with discredit the longer it evades the truth, and that truth is that what it needs is not an architects' charter but a massively funded programme of research and development along the lines of the Apollo, Concorde, Airbus or Eurofighter programmes. To savour the journey that must be travelled, Brenda and Robert Vale's *Green Architecture* (London, 1991) and Sophia and Stefan Behling's *Sol Power: the Evolution of Solar Architecture* (Munich, 1996) are highly recommended.

2 The useful term 'inclusivism' for architectural design embracing every conceivable stylistic tendency was invented by Raymond Moxley, architect of the 1986 Chelsea Harbour development in West London.

3 Patrick Geddes's books *City Development* (1904) and *Cities in Evolution* (1915) are among the most utopian in the early planning lexicon. Geddes called for regional development planning to be integrated with social and economic policy in a manner later attempted in the Soviet Union and the countries of the Eastern bloc.

4 See the author's 'Exogenous Shock', *Architectural Review*, No. 1123, September 1990, for a more detailed account of the repercussions of this event.

5 This comparison was first made by Sam Webb, Professor of Architecture at Canterbury College of Art.

6 The term 'new and organized surface of the earth' was used by the architect Yona Friedman at the Folkestone Experimental Architecture Conference of 1966. Friedman, who designed various megastructure projects in Paris during the 1960s, correctly saw them as representing the pinnacle of achievement of the Modern Movement.

7 The connection between North Sea offshore technology and British 'High-Tech' architecture is discussed in the author's *Theory and Design in the Second Machine Age* (1991).

8 The authority of this volume is somewhat marred by the author's insistence that the 'High-Tech' era ended in 1986 with the explosion of the NASA Space Shuttle 'Challenger'.

9 This account is based on a contemporaneous report filed by the author (who was present) for *The Guardian*.

7 FROM POSTMODERNISM TO TERRORISM

1 This was the celebrated incident of political espionage involving the bugging of the Democratic Party headquarters in Washington DC in 1972 that led to the resignation of Republican president Richard Nixon.

2 This being a reference to Quinlan Terry's extravagantly admired 1988 Richmond Riverside development: modern offices in Georgian dress.

3 Delusions about transparency and reflectivity still dog architecture, but as far as aviation is concerned the matter was settled in the Great War of 1914–18. From the outset the German army was particularly concerned about the high visibility of its large bombing aircraft, the R-planes (*Riesenflugzeug*, or giant aircraft). After attempts at conventional camouflage had failed, transparency was attempted. The airframe of the Linke-Hofmann R.1 of 1917 was covered in transparent celluloid, but reflections spoiled the effect. A second Linke-Hofmann giant bomber, the R.II of 1918, was built in the shape of a small two-seater single engine biplane, but with a wing span of 42 metres, a crew of six and four engines coupled to drive a single propeller. The intention was that enemy aircraft and anti-aircraft guns would miscalculate their aim, thinking the huge machine was nearer than it was. The war ended before the deception could be put to the test. Haddow and Grosz, *The German Giants* (London, 1962).

4 The information about modern 'stealth' aircraft used here, though not the basic comparison with architecture, is drawn from Douglas Richardson, *Stealth Warplanes: Deception, Evasion and Concealment in the Air* (Guild Publishing, 1989).

5 'Not the last word', *Architecture New York*, No. 2, September/October 1993.

6 Asked the purpose of the small conning tower at the apex of the No.1 Poultry building, Sir James replied, 'What is the purpose of the radiator mascot on the front of a car?' *Architecture New York* (*op. cit.*).

7 'Today our materials are conventional but thanks to computers our 3-D geometry is already revolutionary. The morphology of materials might make real dynamism possible in a few years. We shall see. It will depend

on our young architects.' Cecil Balmond, Ove Arup & Partners, 'The Arup Archipelago', *World Architecture*, No. 57, June 1997.

8 This attitude surfaced repeatedly during the Prince of Wales's 1980s crusade for traditional architecture. According to *The Sunday Times* (24 September 1989), no less than 85 per cent of a carefully weighted poll sample of 2,009 adults were in favour of the proposition 'Architects should concentrate on designing buildings that the majority of people find attractive', while 58 per cent agreed that 'All modern architecture is an eyesore'.

9 'An ABECEDARIO of Jean Nouvel', *World Architecture*, No. 31, September 1994.

10 R. Buckminster Fuller, *50 Years of the Design Science Revolution and the World Game*, World Resources Inventory, Philadelphia, 1969.

11 'Miniskirts are Back', *Vogue*, September 1997.

12 The original source of the famous Mies van der Rohe quote is uncertain. The quote from Le Corbusier is found in M. Besset, *Qui était Le Corbusier?* (Geneva, 1968).

13 An excellent source for the effects of communal violence on architecture and planning in Northern Ireland is Paul Stollard, 'The Architecture of No-Man's Land', *Architects' Journal*, 1 August 1984.

14 *Frieze*, September 1994.

8 THE URBANIZATION OF THE SAND-HEAP

1 'Interesting idea isn't it?' Interview with Glenn Murcutt, *World Architecture*, No. 49, September 1996.

2 'Soleri's Laboratory', *World Architecture*, No. 21, January 1993.

3 Asian Development Bank Annual Report 1997, ADB, PO Box 789, 0980 Manila, Philippines.

4 Glenn Murcutt interview, *World Architecture* (*op. cit.*).

5 In 1938 Albert Einstein endorsed Richard Buckminster Fuller's first book *Nine Chains to the Moon*. Until he did so the publishers, Lippincott, had refused to include three chapters dealing with Einstein's theories. According to Fuller, Einstein praised him as follows: 'Young man, I cannot conceive anything I have ever done as having the slightest practical application. I evolved all this work in the hope that it would be of use to cosmogonists and astrophysicists . . . But you appear to have found practical applications for it.' Seven years later Einstein endorsed Le Corbusier's *Le Modulor*, describing it as 'a proportional system that will make the good easy and the bad difficult'.

6 Vilém Flusser, 'Three Times', *Art Forum*, February 1991.

7 'Cheaper tourists clogging streets', *The Times*, 13 January 1997.

8 'Empty government offices could cost taxpayers £500 million', *The Times*, 6 June 1997. Later in the year this embarrassment led the government to propose housing young homeless people in Admiralty Arch, the prestigious former headquarters of the Royal Navy in Trafalgar Square.

9 'Spending on IT soars as Millennium approaches', *The Financial Times*, 12 February 1997.

10 'Destination Airport', British Airways *Business Life*, September 1997.

11 Vilém Flusser, 'Line and Surface', *Main Currents*, New York, January 1973.

12 Interview with Toyo Ito, *Architecture New York*, September 1994.

13 'Soleri's Laboratory', *World Architecture* (see note 2).

14 Howard Odum, *Environment, Power and Society*, Wiley-Interscience, 1971.

15 Mary Fogarty, 'Shop around for home nutrition', *Medical Interface*, January 1996.

16 William Southwood is director of Ove Arup & Partners, London. The quote is from his contribution to *Arups on Engineering* (Ernst & Sohn, 1997).

Southwood is a leading proponent of intelligent buildings. He has also shrewdly observed that ideas of place and space can be heavily influenced by information: 'The office buildings at Stockley Park near Heathrow airport have a central London telephone prefix so that potential tenants can believe they are in London.'

9 TERMINAL ARCHITECTURE

1 'You can be the master of potential disaster', Business Continuity Supplement, *The Times*, 6 February 1997.
2 'Architecture as an anti-technological virus: the work of Michael Trudgeon', *World Architecture*, No. 23, May 1993. See also 'World Hyper Kitchen', dealing with roll-in, roll-out kitchens for the conversion of redundant office buildings into apartments, *World Architecture*, No. 35, March 1995.
3 Antoine de Saint Exupéry, *Wind, Sand and Stars* (1942). Saint Exupéry's comments on technology are extremely insightful. The complete passage, referring to the evolution of the aeroplane, reads, 'Startling as it is that all visible evidence of invention should have been refined out of this instrument and that there should be delivered to us an object as natural as a pebble polished by the waves, it is equally wonderful that he who uses this instrument should be able to forget that it is a machine. Every machine will lose its identity in function.'
4 The role of the architects involved in the design of the Minworth distribution centre was typically negative. They saw their task as 'scaling down' the 20-metre-high by 240-metre-long building. This they did by adding huge purple panels, big gold Cadbury signs and Trabant-style styling strips to the 55,000-square-metre surface of its sandwich panel walls.
5 'And they all look just the same. . .', *The Observer*, 8 May 1994.
6 A notable example being Peter Buchanan of the magazine *Architectural Review*, who closed many lectures in the early 1990s with remarks to this effect.
7 Sources for Toyo Ito's quotes are *El Croquis*, No. 71, Madrid, 1995; *World Architecture*, No. 43, February 1996; and *World Architecture*, No. 53, February 1997.
8 The Virtual Architecture Partnership was formed in 1993 to explore the field of spatially disruptive design. The partners were Peter Wislocki and the author. The only fully designed project was the Milton Keynes 'Futureworld' competition entry (with Tony Keller), which was unplaced. The theme park proposal formed the subject of discussions with Peter Gabriel's Real World Studios group and with AVE Realization Ltd. The 'black-box' office building study was proposed informally to Ove Arup & Partners in 1995 as a suitable subject for funding by the Arup Foundation. The outline specification called for a very high-efficiency air-conditioned sealed urban commercial building, capable of operating in very poor air conditions with the capacity to reprocess its air if necessary. This building would have operated with lights out for video monitor work and would in effect have been 'glassless architecture', with the loss of direct visual contact with the outside world made good by high-definition moving images of 'natural scenery' projected inside.
9 Notably the famous Ruskin versus Whistler trial of 1877. See Gaunt, *The Aesthetic Adventure* (op. cit.).
10 Quoted in Kurt Lustenberger, *Adolf Loos* (1994).

Bibliography

Arups on Engineering (Ernst & Sohn, 1997)

Baker, William, *A History of the Marconi Company* (London, 1970)

Behling, Sophia and Stefan Behling, *Sol Power: The Evolution of Solar Architecture* (Munich, 1996)

Besset, M., *Qui était Le Corbusier?* (Geneva, 1968)

Betjeman, John, *Ghastly Good Taste* (London, 1933)

Buckminster Fuller, Richard, *50 Years of the Design Science Revolution and the World Game*, World Resources Inventory (Philadelphia, 1969)

'Canary Wharf: a landmark in construction', supplement to *Building*, October 1991

Clausewitz, Karl von, *On War* (London, 1977). Original German language edition 1831

Davies, Colin, *High-Tech Architecture* (London, 1987)

Energy-Conscious Design: A Primer for Architects. Commission of the European Communities, incorporating the proceedings of the Third European Conference on Solar Energy and Urban Planning, Florence 1993 (London, 1994)

Gaunt, William, *The Aesthetic Adventure* (London, 1945)

Geddes, Patrick, *City Development* (London, 1904)

—, *Cities in Evolution* (London, 1915)

Glendinning, Miles and Stefan Muthesius, *Tower Block* (London, 1994)

Haddow, G. W. and Peter M. Grosz, *The German Giants* (London, 1962)

Handy, Charles, *The Future of Work* (Oxford, 1984)

Howard, Ebenezer, *Tomorrow: A Peaceful Path to Real Reform* (London, 1898)

Jencks, Charles, *The Language of Postmodern Architecture* (1976)

Kubler, George, *The Shape of Time* (London, 1962)

Lethaby, William, *Architecture, Mysticism and Myth* (London, 1892)

Loos, Adolf, *Spoken into the Void: Collected Essays* (London, 1982)

Lustenberger, Kurt, *Adolf Loos* (Zurich, 1994)

Marriott, Oliver, *The Property Boom* (London, 1967)

McLuhan, Marshall, *Understanding Media* (London, 1964)

Metcalf, Thomas, *An Imperial Vision* (London, 1989)

Pawley, Martin, *Architecture versus Housing* (London, 1971)

—, *Buckminster Fuller* (London, 1990)

—, *Theory and Design in the Second Machine Age* (Oxford, 1991)

Prak, Niels, *Architects: The Noted and the Ignored* (New York, 1984)

Richards, James, *Architectural Criticism in the 1930s*, monograph, Architectural Press (London, 1962)

Richardson, Douglas, *Stealth Warplanes: Deception, Evasion and Concealment in the Air* (London, 1989)

Saint Exupéry, Antoine de, *Wind, Sand and Stars*, published in translation in the anthology *Airman's Odyssey* (New York, 1942)

Save Britain's Heritage, 'From Splendour to Banality: The Rebuilding of the City of London', pamphlet, 1983

Scruton, Roger, 'Art History and Aesthetic Judgement', in *The Classical Vernacular* (London, 1994)

Sullivan, Louis Henry, *The Autobiography of an Idea* (New York, 1924)

Vale, Brenda and Robert Vale, *Green Architecture* (London, 1991)

Willey, T. R., *The Early Renaissance* (London, 1955)

List of Illustrations

All illustrations otherwise uncredited are by the author.